Hogarth, Walpole and Commercial Britain

HOGARTH, WALPOLE AND COMMERCIAL BRITAIN

David Dabydeen

A Hansib Publication

First published in 1987 by Hansib Publishing Limited

© David Dabydeen 1987

Cover illustration: William Hogarth's *A Rake's Progress* (Frame 5) (Reproduced by courtesy of The Trustees of Sir John Soane's Museum, London).

ISBN 1 870518 45 4

Produced by Hansib Publishing Limited, 139/149 Fonthill Road, London N4 3HF, Tel: 01 281 1191
Printed in England by: Hansib Printing Limited, Unit 19, Caxton Hill Industrial Estate, Hertfordshire, Tel: 0992 553592

To Anna Rutherford, Sally and David Tonkinson, Sandra and Jai Latiff.

TABLE OF CONTENTS

PREFACE   11

HOGARTH AND THE SOUTH SEA BUBBLE   15
    1. *The South Sea Scheme*   21
    2. *The Lottery*   40
    3. *Masquerades and Operas*   42
    4. *Royalty, Episcopacy and Law*   49
    5. *The Mystery of Masonry*   52
    6. *Cunicularii*   57
    7. References to the South Sea Bubble elsewhere in
       Hogarth's work   59

A HARLOT'S PROGRESS
    1. References to the South Sea Bubble in Hogarth's
       two 'Progresses' of the 1730s   73
    2. The South Sea Bubble compared with the Charitable
       Corporation frauds   88
    3. *A Harlot's Progress* as political allegory   91

APPENDIX 1: WILLIAM HOGARTH'S PORTRAIT OF
              GEORGE AUGUSTUS   151

SELECTED BIBLIOGRAPHY   160

LIST OF ILLUSTRATIONS   162

INDEX   164

Preface

This book addresses William Hogarth's first major series of prints, *A Harlot's Progress* (1732), and argues that they contain elements of *political* satire directed against the régime of Sir Robert Walpole. The conventional reading of the series as humorous moral satire has endured from Hogarth's time to today. The overwhelming consensus of critical opinion is that Hogarth, apart from early prints like *Royalty, Episcopacy, and Law* (1724) and *Henry the Eighth and Anne Boleyn* (1728/9), did not dabble in politics until late in his career. Ronald Paulson sees a dramatic change in Hogarth's political output from 1728, the early prints being 'the last tangible evidence of Hogarth's reaction to politics until the mid-1750s'. Derek Jarrett emphasises Hogarth's political neutrality and the generalized nature of his early satires, whilst M. Dorothy George writes that 'after 1724 none of his prints conform to the anti-ministerial convention'.[1] These views, then, presume a discontinuity in Hogarth's political concerns with the appearance of *A Harlot's Progress*. In proposing a political reading of *A Harlot's Progress*, and to a lesser extent, *A Rake's Progress*, my argument is not only that they have been profoundly misunderstood but that the consistency and continuity of Hogarth's early work have not been properly recognised.

In attempting to reveal this consistency I begin with an examination of the *South Sea Scheme* (1721), one of Hogarth's earliest prints. Scholars of the eighteenth century have argued the momentousness of the South Sea episode and its long term effects on the economic, as well as the literary and intellectual, life of Britain. George Sherburn for instance has written that the change of eighteenth century attitudes to commerce, from the early enthusiasm of critics like Defoe and Young to the later pessimism of Goldsmith, Blake and Cowper, and then the condemnation of commerce by Crabbe, Wordsworth and the Romantics, was due to the 'long-term chastening effects' of the South Sea Bubble which caused 'a widespread revulsion from the merchantilist worship of commerce to the physiocratic idea that wealth comes basically from the soil'.[2] Given the importance of the South Sea episode it is surprising that Hogarth scholars should have paid such scant attention to his *South Sea Scheme*. The print has been neglected by scholars who have seldom devoted more than a couple of paragraphs to explaining its meaning. Austin Dobson considered it to be 'confused' and 'obscure', echoing Horace Walpole who dismissed it as 'a very poor performance'.[3] Even Paulson in his monumental biography of the artist deals with the print in a general way, not looking closely at its content. Nor has there been any recognition of the pervasive influence of the South Sea episode on Hogarth's thinking, although Jack Lindsay did correctly assert, but without proper elaboration, that the South Sea disaster was 'an occasion that deeply stirred his judgement of this world.'[4] After attempting a minute examination of Hogarth's *South Sea Scheme* I trace South Sea motifs in his other early works – *The Lottery* (1721), *Masquerades and Operas* (1723/4), *Royalty, Episcopacy, and Law* (1724), *The Mystery of Masonry* (1724) and *Cunicularii* (1726) – and I interpret these prints in the context of public thought about the South Sea Bubble. A hitherto unknown version of Hogarth's print, *His Royal Highness George Prince of Wales* (1720?) is discussed in an appendix.

Having established the thematic unity of the prints of the 1720s, their interplay of ideas and interests – facts insufficiently, sometimes hardly, recognised by Hogarth scholars – I turn to the memories of the South Sea Bubble in Hogarth's work of the 1730s, specifically *A Harlot's Progress* and *A Rake's Progress*. By this time Sir Robert Walpole had come to be associated with the South Sea scandal. Reference to the Bubble became a recognisable feature of anti-Walpole satire. The Bubble symbolized the spirit of material and moral corruption that was seen as the distinguishing mark of Walpole's reign. The two Progresses are read as anti-Walpole satire, their representation of corruption interpreted in the light of anti-Walpole literature of the 1720s and 1730s.

This book started life as a doctoral dissertation undertaken at University College, London. I am grateful to Dr Keith Walker for supervising the dissertation with such care and to Professor John Dixon Hunt and Mr Robin Simon, my examiners, for their valuable criticism. I am grateful to Professor Ronald Paulson for his monumental studies on Hogarth and for the opportunity of discussing my work with him. Critics of Paulson have attacked him on the basis that his method is *a priori*, that it consists of searching through prints for just those details which can be construed in support of his thesis. Every similarity becomes a source, and every source a quotation or allusion or reference. They have accused him of 'over-reading', of finding narrative everywhere, and of barking up the wrong trees.

But Hogarth himself challenges us to speculate and to indulge in a hectic chase after meaning. He invites us to unlock his narrative puzzles and sees this as providing essential intellectual fun for the interpreter of his work. Hence in the caption to his *South Sea Scheme*, having explained for us some of the details of the print, he concludes, 'Guess at the Rest you find out more'. He dares us to find out more, to discover his intentions. To Hogarth, 'barking up the wrong trees' is a necessary adventure.

Naturally there is a risk involved in the 'guessing', a risk of ingenuity of interpretation. Let us not forget however that Hogarth revelled in being called 'The Ingenious Mr Hogarth'. Not to 'guess' is to risk settling for the obvious or conventional meaning.

The difficulties over how to interpret Hogarth are further compounded when we seek to reveal *political* nuances in his work. Paul Langford, writing about political expression in the age of Walpole tells of how people interpreted political meaning in the seemingly most innocuous word or emblem.[5] Jacobite plots and counterplots, real or alleged, created a political environment of deep suspicion in which signification thrived:

> conspiracy and fear of conspiracy bred a morbid interest in the strange world of the plotter and the spy and added a sinister dimension to the political vocabulary. Codes, cryptograms, symbols, took on additional meaning, and occasionally nature seemed positively to imitate art. Thus, the strange evidence produced against those involved in the Atterbury Plot in 1722 caused great public interest in the hidden significance of an apparently innocuous vocabulary, and furnished Swift with an effective scene in *Gulliver's Travels*. In Lagado Gulliver found a 'set of artists of dexterity sufficient to find out the mysterious Meanings of Words, Syllables, and Letters'. Anagrams and acrostics abounded and absurdly everyday phrases turned out to have important political meanings. A sieve signified a court lady, a lame dog, an invalid...a chamber-pot, a committee of grandees. No parody of Swift's could have exceeded the absurdities of reality, nor did the cryptic nature of much graphic satire seem to contemporaries in the least fanciful.

Given such limitlessness of signification and interpretation, today's scholars can legitimately (indeed, they are *bound* to) take risks in their deconstruction of graphic satire in the age of Walpole. Such was the vogue for attacking Walpole that any work which criticized the morality of the nation was interpreted by contemporaries as criticizing Walpole: the reception of Swift's *Gulliver's Travels* and Gay's *Beggar's Opera* as anti-Walpole satire is proof of this eagerness to find political meaning everywhere (irrespective of the intentions of the authors). Artists used Walpole as a convenient symbol of corruption and would include him in their prints, irrespective of his actual relevance to the satire. For instance, *B. M. Satires* No. 2465 (1741), an engraving of Vauxhall Gardens, in which Walpole is 'worked into this otherwise innocent sexual satire'.[6]

In this book I attempt to hazard a 'guess at the rest'; to speculate on the political references in his work which to my mind constitute a part of 'the rest'. This is not to quarrel with conventional responses to works like *A Harlot's Progress* which dwell on its humour, its bawdy, its moralistic tone, etc., etc., but rather to agree with J.H. Plumb when he states that Hogarth's work is open to a variety of simultaneous interpretations which can co-exist happily, even in seeming contradiction of each other:

> Hogarth's engravings spoke to audiences at different levels, from the sophisticated to the naive: for the former there was a complicated moral message, made

intriguing by obvious clues that those with inside knowledge could read, and for the latter a single truth, obvious to all, that the wages of sin are death.[7]

Notes

1. R. Paulson: *Hogarth: His Life, Art and Times* (2 vols, New Haven, 1971), Vol 1, p. 174; D. Jarrett: *The Ingenious Mr Hogarth* (London, 1976), p. 65f; M. Dorothy George: *English Political Caricature to 1972* (Oxford, 1959), p. 113.

2. Tom K Meier in his doctoral dissertation *Defoe and the Defence of Commerce*, Columbia University, 1971, pp 14-15, discusses Sherburn's views.

3. A. Dobson: *William Hogarth* (London, 1907), pp 15-16; J. Nichols: *Biographical Anecdotes of William Hogarth* (London, 1781), p.67.

4. J. Lindsay: *Hogarth. His Art and his World* (London, 1977), p. 18.

5. Paul Langford: *Walpole and the Robinocracy* (Cambridge, 1986), p. 16.

6. *Ibid.*, p. 22.

7. J. Plumb: 'Hogarth's Progress', in *The New York Review of Books*, 16/12/1971.

Hogarth and the South Sea Bubble

Brokerage was not a phenomenon new to the eighteenth century. As far back as 1376 we find the term being used, in the Parliamentary decree that 'No stranger-merchant, nor other stranger, shall use or exercise the occupation of "brocage" between merchant and merchant, or other persons, nor be a "broceur" within the City of London or its suburbs'.[1] In the last decade of the sixteenth century there were thirty brokers in the City of London, controlled by the Lord Mayor and Aldermen. Speculation in stocks however, as opposed to market commodities like corn, cloth or land, only took off at the end of the seventeenth century, by which time the number of middlemen has risen to hundreds. It was at this time too that the stockjobber acquired an odious reputation. The newspapers of the day carried accounts of his trickery, the sort of fraudulence which caused widespread resentment among merchants and which led to the 1697 Act seeking to regulate the practice of brokerage. The stockjobber began to appear in literature as a figure to be satirized: in Thomas Shadwell's *The Volunteers, or The Stock-Jobbers* (1693), Nickum the card-cheat describes them as 'Rogues... worse than us Sharpers with Bars and false Boxes'. The projects satirized in Shadwell's play, like the mouse-trap for clearing the kingdom of vermin, or the scheme for conveying messages underwater, especially useful in wintry weather when the ice is too thin to travel on, look forward to some of the real Bubble projects of 1720 in their absurdity.

Two tracts published in the first year of the new century expressed the anxiety over stockjobbing activity that was building up in the later years of the seventeenth century. The first, *The Freeholders Plea Against Stock-Jobbing Elections Of Parliament Men*, describes the new strange type of businessman whose sole concern is with profit-making, regardless of all other criteria, moral or patriotic. The question whether 'Stock will rise upon 't' totally conditions his attitude to national and international events. His attitude is all the more dangerous because of his increasing control over Parliamentary representation: the tract's main complaint is against the way Parliamentary seats are 'Jobb'd upon Exchange for Mony, and Transfer'd like *East-India* Stock, to those who bid most' (p.10). The fact that these profiteers could control such a source of authority and power poses a threat to the nation's welfare:

> The *French* King need not keep great Armies on Foot, Build Ships, and Strengthen himself at Sea to Ruin us, if the great Affairs of the Kingdom concerted in Parliament should come to be prepar'd, manag'd, and bypass'd at *Garraway's* and *Jonathan's* Coffee-house, and expos'd to Sale by a parcel of Stock-Jobbers. (p.20)

It is this sense of the threat to the nation which is the main feature of the second tract, *The Villany Of Stock-Jobbers Detected*, attributed to Defoe. It deals with 'that new *Mistery* or *Machine* of Trade we call *Stock-Jobbing*'. The power of the stockjobbers lies in their ability to manipulate the market so that by their strange magic 'the Price shall dance attendance on their designs, and rise and fall as they please, without any regard to the Intrinsick worth of the Stock' (p.5). The mechanics of their operation are beyond the comprehension of both writers: "Twoud puzzle a good *Logician* to make it out by *Syllogism*', the first writer declares. Defoe's response to their trickery is darker; there is something fearful and sinister about the whole business:

> The War they manage is carried on with worse Weapons than Swords and Musquets; Bombs may Fire our Towns, and Troops over run and plunder us; But these People can ruin Men silently, undermine and impoverish by a sort of impenetrable Artifice, like Poison that works at a distance, can wheedle Men to ruin themselves, and *Fiddle them out of their Money*, by the strange and unheard of Engines of *Interests, Discounts, Transfers, Tallies, Debentures, Shares, Projects*, and the *Devil and all* of Figures and hard Names. (pp. 21-2)

The language becomes almost religious in tone, rises to a pitch of horror, conveying a sense of apocalyptic destruction which is all the more frightening because it is incomprehensible:

> They can draw their Armies and levy Troops, set *Stock* against *Stock, Company* against *Company, Alderman* against *Alderman,* and the poor Passive Trades men, like the Peasant in *Flanders,* are plundered by both Sides, and hardly knows who hurts them. (p.22)

The atmosphere of superstition generated by the collapse of the South Sea Scheme in 1720, which accounts for the presence of the Devil in satirical Bubble prints and literature, is understandable in this earlier context of feelings about unseen powers at work.

What is interesting about these two tracts is the new and frightened awareness of the power of moneyed men whose tyranny is of a new order, mysterious and unseen. They are not merely wicked Jewish types demanding a pound of flesh from some unfortunate individual, but they have the power to bleed a whole state. Their poison is not like that of Marlowe's Jew, of a known chemistry; it is 'Poison that works at a distance'. Moreover they are not so easily controllable by the Law since Parliament is in their subjection. After the collapse of the South Sea Scheme two decades later, people were to voice similar feelings about great criminals above the reach of the Law, screened by the Authorities. The realization of the possibility that six or eight men could combine to form a powerful body, with the aim of manipulating stock by buying and selling among themselves, anticipates in a striking way the later manipulation of the market by the South Sea Directors as well as the tremendous control these Directors, whose favours were courted even by the Nobility, wielded over the Nation. In 1720, Erasmus Lewis was to write of the power of such a combination:

> the least discerning eye can discover that a body of men, with a stock of forty-three millions, and credit for as much more, acting by united counsels, must fill the House of Commons, and rule this little world... What occasion will there be for Parliaments hereafter?[2]

Defoe's view, in 1701, that stockjobbers possessed the ability 'to declare a new sort of Civil War among us when they please' can hardly be dismissed as hysterical.

In the summer of 1720, when trading in South Sea stock was tempestuous, Hogarth's finances must have been at a low water-mark. His father had not long ago died, in May 1718, and his uncle Edmund who may have contributed something towards the relief of his poor relations died in 1719 leaving a mere shilling in his will for Hogarth's mother. The male responsibility for the family of three women now rested with William who, from the way he provided for his sisters later in life, must have had a strong sense of his obligations. His break with Ellis Gamble in 1720 was probably to help out in his mother's little millinery business and at the same time to start earning some money of his own. He was approaching 23 years of age, and his only achievements so far were mostly the engravings on silver done as Gamble's apprentice. His immediate prospects were commissions for business cards and other such ephemera, but his ambitions were strong enough for him to join the St Martin's Lane Academy in October 1720. Leaving Gamble was a gamble in itself. Finding the two guineas subscription fees for the Academy with which to speculate on his future must have been a desperate task, whereas others had been subscribing to worthless projects, wagering, winning or wasting thousands in Exchange Alley: no doubt Hogarth would have recognised with much bitterness the parallel between his situation and that of South Sea speculators.[3]

The experience of his father would have been uppermost in his mind, especially now that he was setting up shop and having to think of finding patrons and dealing with printsellers. In his autobiographical writings, he tells of leaving Gamble, of becoming master of his own time, and mentions the premature death of his father, 'occasioned partly by the treatment he met with from this set of people [i.e. booksellers], and partly by disappointment from great men's promises'.[4] In the autumn of 1720, one of these great men was alive and well and enjoying the prospect of a return to power – Robert Harley, Chief Minister between 1710-14, founder and first Governor of the South Sea Company. Harley had fallen in 1714 at the death of Queen Anne and the Whig ascendancy that accompanied the enthronement of George I, but with the Whig administration threatened by the collapse of the South Sea Scheme, the possibility of a political comeback by Harley was on the cards. It was to Harley that Richard Hogarth had written, in 1710, seeking patronage. He had submitted to him a proposal to solve the National Debt, with no success.[5] Now, in 1720, with South Sea activity at its peak, and with men making private fortunes from the Scheme to clear the National Debt, Hogarth's bitterness over the imprisonment of his father for debt and his death in poverty would have intensified.

Nevertheless, despite the fate of his father, Hogarth was at this stage intent on seeking out the favours of 'great men' since it was the only course open to an unknown artist like himself. It was too early, and he was too poor, to have the confidence to deal directly with the public, as he did in the next decade. Hence his first major engraving, *An Allegory of George, Prince of Wales as the Future Protector of the Realm* (*Figure 1*) bears all the hallmarks of flattery.[6] The print appears to refer

Figure 1: William Hogarth: *An Allegory of George, Prince of Wales*

to the peace made between George I and the Prince of Wales in April 1720, which was stage-managed by politicians and business interests, not for any Christian ideal of family reconciliation but for political and economic reasons. The ruling politicians hoped that by uniting King and Prince they would ensure their survival in office after the death of the one and the enthronement of the other. The businessmen hoped that the value of South Sea stock would escalate by creating a sense of Royal unity which was to reinforce the propaganda they disseminated about the South Sea Company acting as an agent of peace, bringing the people together in one common patriotic and profitable endeavour. Hungerford for instance had tried to justify the Directors in September 1720, after the collapse of the price of stocks, by declaring that:

> They have done more than the Crown, the Pulpit and the Magistrates could do: for they have reconciled all Parties in one common interest and thereby laid asleep, if not wholly extinguished, our Domestic Jars and Animosity.[7]

Pope was to echo, with heavy irony, Sir John Blunt's own beliefs, as expressed in the latter's tract *A True State of the South Sea Scheme* (1722), written to justify the South Sea Directors:

> No mean Court-badge, great Scriv'ner! fir'd thy brain,
> Nor lordly Luxury, nor City Gain:
> No, 'twas thy righteous end, asham'd to see
> Senates degen'rate, Patriots disagree,
> And nobly wishing Party-rage to cease,
> To buy both sides, and give thy Country peace.
> (*Epistle to Bathurst*, 1.147f.)

That the Royal reconciliation was bogus, achieved by bribes to both parties in the form of South Sea stock, was of course known to all those involved in Court affairs; they were a few seditious broadsheets hinting at this, but they were quickly suppressed.[8] Hogarth's innate scepticism about the motives and activities of 'great men', fuelled by the remembrance of his father's treatment, would probably have made him aware of its dubious foundation. Nevertheless, his work chooses to reflect the point of view of the Authorities rather than that of the Opposition cynics.

His picture depicts Peace sitting on the collapsed instruments of war, a cannon, a shield and a sword, and holding up to the medallion of the Prince of Wales an olive branch. Hercules stands triumphantly over the dead Hydra of discord. The three Graces offer the Prince power, and patronage of the Arts and of Commerce. The pile of money and goods at the feet of the kneeling Grace refers to the possibility of great national wealth, a healing wealth, such as the South Sea Company seemed to offer in 1720. In the background is a hint of a thriving city, the smoke rising from it indicating industry. It co-exists harmoniously with Nature, with the countryside. Hogarth is perhaps referring here to the reconciliation between the Whigs, representatives of the City and of Commerce, and the Tories, of the landed interest, a reconciliation that the South Sea Scheme appeared to effect. The Company, deeply involved in Whig politics in 1720, was after all the brain-child of the Tories. Members of both factions and sub-factions had large investments in the Company. Nobility and tradesmen rubbed shoulders in Exchange Alley or shook hands on completion of deals. The Gentry sold their estates to travel to London to purchase stock, and successful City-men bought up land and retired to the country.[9]

If the *Allegory of George, Prince of Wales* was an attempt to exploit the optimistic mood of the Spring of 1720 then the *South Sea Scheme* (*Figure 2*) was to make capital out of the collapse of the Scheme and the enormous popular discontent in the country. The two prints are very opposite in mood and style. In the first, the occasion of order and reconciliation is appropriately conveyed by the symmetry and coherent structure of forms. All attention is centred on the portrait of the Prince. The Graces beckon to him from the left, Peace and

Figure 2: William Hogarth:
The South Sea Scheme

Britannia from the right. In the centre stands the upright figure of Hercules, uniting the two groups: he is turned towards the group on the left but his left hand gestures to the right. Hogarth, at the outset of his career, his ambition being to paint in the grand style of the successful Thornhill, displays here his working knowledge of the principles of History Painting – the dignity of mood, the arrangement of gestures and motions into a coherent and idealized whole, the employment of Classical motifs and personages. The *South Sea Scheme* by contrast is scattered and unfocussed, reflecting the actual confusion that preceded and followed the bursting of the South Sea Bubble. Its pickpocket, shoeblack, whore, and gambler, belong more to the realm of Genre. More important is the incipient feeling for the natural anarchic energy of the crowd, the confusion and complexity of purpose and action that form the rhythm of real life, as opposed to the stylized rhythm of History Painting. It is true that the crowd in the *South Sea Scheme* still retains a planned quality, that some of its activity is emblematic rather than realistic, but there is all the same an awareness of the natural tempo of life that anticipates the depiction of crowds in Hogarth's later works.

The two events of 1720 then, both relating to the affairs of the South Sea Company, provided Hogarth, at the very beginning of his vocation as an independent artist, with the opportunity of experimenting in two contrasting styles, the idealization of History painting and the realism of Genre. The rest of his career can be summarized by reference to this choice between the two styles, to the way he adapts one to the other and vehemently justifies the validity of the resulting product against the scorn and suspicion of the connoisseurs. It was also a momentous time in so far as the South Sea débâcle helped to shape Hogarth's perceptions about the nature and influence of money. The *South Sea Scheme* contains the seeds of future Hogarthian themes, and motifs that recur in later works. It demonstrates his ability to assimilate current thought and to present them visually, for details in his picture echo or summarize many of the opinions thrown out by the mass of satirical prints and literature dealing with the Mississippi and South Sea Schemes.

1. The South Sea Scheme (1721)

(a) Religious Corruption:

By changing the inscription on the Monument (instead of the Papists and the Fire of London, the new reference is to disaster resulting from the Bubble) Hogarth indicates that the nation's destruction is due to more baser forces than religious differences. Hogarth may have borrowed the idea of changing the inscription from a pack of cards upon the 1688 Revolution, the 2 of Clubs of which depicts 'The Inscription taken out of ye Monument' by subversive Jacobites – Hogarth's point being that Finance and not Religion and Politics is the new cause of civil disturbance.[10] Financial concerns had replaced the struggle for religious integrity as the catalyst of social and political action not only in 1720 but in the eighteenth century as a whole. By the juxtaposition of St Paul's and the Monument on the right hand side of the print Hogarth points to the Church's involvement in South Sea affairs and to the way Business was propped up and sanctified by theology. Swift in his *Argument against Abolishing Christianity* (1708) had satirized the links between the Church and the Moneyed Interests by mentioning the unfavourable effects on Capital should nominal Christianity be abolished: 'I do very much apprehend that in six months' time after the Act is passed for the extirpation of the Gospel the Bank and East India stock may fall at least one per cent'. Not surprisingly the stockjobbing of 1720 produced similar satire on religion. In *The Yea and Nea Stock-Jobbers, or The 'Change-Alley Quakers Anatomiz'd* (London, 1720), the poet exposes to ridicule the casuistry of the clergy, the way involved religious arguments were employed to justify profiteering in South Sea stock. It was indeed true that top clergymen were involved in Bubble speculation. The Archbishop of York, who invested £1,000 in South Sea stock is one among many priests whose names are to be found in the Subscription Lists.[11]

The character of Sir John Blunt, Director of the South Sea Company and architect of its vast success in the summer of 1720 symbolised this unholy alliance of God and Mammon. He was the type of man who kept the Sabbath and anything else he could lay his hands on. He lived his life 'with a prayer-book in his right hand and a prospectus in his left hand…never letting his right hand know what his left hand was doing'.[12] His religiosity to some extent motivated his capitalist enterprise. Pope was to describe him as 'A Dissenter of a most religious deportment', and Toland mentioned the prophet-like quality of his deliverances:

> He visibly affected a prophetick stile, delivering his words with an emphasis and extraordinary vehemence: and us'd to put himself into a commanding posture, rebuking those that durst in the least oppose any thing he said, and endeavouring to inculcate, as if what he spoke was by impulse, uttering these and such like expressions:
> "*Gentlemen, don't be dismayed: You must act with firmness, with resolution, with courage. I tell you, 'tis not a common matter you have before you. The greatest thing in the world is referred to you. All the money of Europe will center amongst you. All the nations of the earth will bring you tribute*".[13]

In Nicholas Amhurst's *An Epistle to Sir John Blunt* (1720) Blunt's ability to create wealth is described in terms calculated to pander to his religious self-esteem:

So Moses smote the barren Rock,
(An Emblem of the South-Sea Stock)

The caption to Hogarth's print reflects upon the Church's neglect of its pastoral duties:

Thus when the Sheepherds are at play,
Their flocks must surely go astray.

It was a common criticism voiced in many of the South Sea satires. The 7 of Diamonds of one pack of Bubble cards depicts three priests dealing in stock, one of them confessing that 'the Care of Stock is better than the care of Souls' (*Figure 3*). J.B.'s *A Poem Occasion'd by the Rise and Fall of South Sea Stock* (1720) exposes the betrayal of the

Figure 3: South Sea Bubble Card

Three Rev'rend Teachers, mutually agree,
To venture just one Thousand in South Sea ;
Thus Stock they bought, by Tyths, turn'd into Gold
And fear twill fetch them, but a Tyth when sold.

common people by their guardians and stewards, including the clergy:

> The Country Pastor leaves his slighted Flocks,
> Hastes to the *Change*, and barters in the Stocks. (p.15)

In Hogarth's print, one clergyman rides the merry-go-round in the company of a whore whose birch will act upon his flesh as a sexual stimulus, not as an instrument of penance and self-chastisement. Another clergyman supervises the breaking of 'Honesty' on a wheel, and a third, a Quaker, plays pitch-and-toss with a Jew and a Catholic, his back turned against St Paul's and the solid Protestant piety that that building signified. This trio of gamblers so earth-bound in their avarice (they are kneeling) are diagonally opposite St Paul's whose dome and cross rise to the heavens. Their kneeling and their spatial position within the picture recall the figures of the three Graces in the previous *Allegory of Prince George* – they are the sordid reality behind the idealism of the earlier print.

The perversion of religious values can be seen in the echoes of the Gospel story: the flogging of 'Honour' recalls the flagellation of Christ, and the three gamblers echo the dicing for Christ's garments. The religious attitude of these gamblers – they kneel as if in devotion, and their hands are clasped as in prayer or placed at the heart in a gesture of piety – also recalls the iconography of the Adoration of the Magi. The new focus of attention however is not on the Christ-child but on the coins. The pitch-and-toss is the new ritual, the new religious ceremony performed under the Guildhall, not St Paul's, and watched over the semi-divine figure of Gog or Magog. Hogarth's view compliments that of the satirists like J.B. who wrote of the 'Sacred Thirst of Gain' and who described the South Sea period as a time

> When Men, grown mad with a Desire of Wealth,
> Forsook their Maker to adore their Pelf,
> No Deity but Gold, their Thoughts inspir'd,
> Nor other God the greedy Saints desir'd.
> (*op. cit.*, p. 4)

In Hogarth's print the loss of religious integrity can be seen also in the alliance of Jew and Christian, both of whom have buried their historical differences to participate in the money game. Hogarth's point is one made elsewhere: 'Religion! why, they don't mind Religion in *Change-Alley*. But *Turks, Jews, Atheists*, and *Infidels*, mingle there as if they were a-kin to one another'.[14] Although their activities were restricted by English Law, Jews were notable businessmen, heavily involved in trading and stock-jobbing; one section of the Royal Exchange was named the 'Jews Walk'. Some of them were great purchasers of stock in 1720, recognisable figures in Exchange Alley (*Figures 4-6*). The Jew was habitually attacked in Bubble prints, poems and plays.[15] His apparent success obviously generated much envy and hatred, hence perhaps the re-publication in 1720 of *The History, Fall and Miserable Ruin of the Jews,* one of the many anti-semitic tracts that appeared periodically throughout the century. Newspaper reports on Jews in 1720 would not have added to their popularity either. At the end of August, a few days before the beginning of the devaluation of South Sea stock, the *Original Weekly Journal* (Saturday, August 27th) tells of the lavishness and splendour of a Jewish wedding: 'There were present to see the Ceremony the greatest Concourse of the Nobility and Gentry that ever was known upon such an Occasion'. On October 10th, in the time of confusion and depression following the collapse of Public Credit and paper currency, the *Daily Post,* which had earlier carried a news item on Jews going from door to door buying up foreign coins, reports on the Jews celebrating their Feast of the Tabernacles.

Figure 4: South Sea Bubble Card

25

Figure 5: South Sea Bubble
Card

Figure 6: South Sea Bubble Card

(b) Social Disorder

Hogarth depicts an ape dressed as a gentleman, an emblem of the social upstart – the ape was a recurring figure in South Sea satire.[16] He shows too a harlot, clergyman, shoeblack and nobleman riding the same merry-go-round, and the print's caption tells of the involvement of all classes in financial speculation, 'from Blue Garters down/To all Blue Aprons in the Town'. It is an observation made in almost every piece of satire on the South Sea Bubble.

> Here Stars and Garters do appear
> Among our Lords, the Rabble,
> To Buy and Sell, to See and Hear
> The Jews and Gentiles squabble.
> (*A South Sea Ballad*, 1720)

In Exchange Alley, 'Lords and Porters undistinguish'd walk', a reference perhaps to Duke, an Exchange Alley porter who was reported to have made £2,000 'by the Bubbles, and is about to set up his Chaise, with a handsome Equipage.'[17] One satire symbolises the utter social chaos by depicting a Gentleman shaking hands respectfully with a *Negro* stockjobber! Of course the Feudal structure had loosened long before 1720, its disintegration effected partly by the gradual rise to power of the moneyed middle class, goldsmiths, merchants, manufacturers and the rest, who profited from the commercial possibilities opened up by the establishment of American colonies, from increased traffic with Europe, and the Indies; partly by the enrichment of the yeomanry from the increased wool trade. The gradual social changes are presented beautifully in the song 'A Beggar got a Beadle':

> A Beggar got a Beadle
>   A Beadle got a Yeoman
> A Yeoman got a Prentice,
>   And a Prentice got a Freeman:
> The Freeman got a Master,
>   The Master got a Lease,
> The Lease made him a Gentleman
>   And Justice of the Peace.
> The Justice being Rich,
>   And Gallant in desire,
> He marry'd with a Lady,
>   And so he got a Squire:
> The Squire got a Knight
>   Of Courage bold and stout;
> The Knight he got a Lord
>   And so it came about.[18]

What the South Sea Bubble seemed to effect, with its possibility of instant wealth, was a speeding up of this gradual process so that beggar became Lord overnight without any of the intermediary changes; as one South Sea poem puts it:

> From a Dunghill to a Coach
> A Rascal rises in a Touch.[19]

It was however a grossly exaggerated attitude: the common people could hardly raise the hundreds of pounds needed to purchase South Sea stock and any profits made from the cheaper subscriptions to other Bubbles would have been much too insubstantial to pose any real threat to the social fabric. It was people of the middle classes, of the financial standing of men like Blunt, who gained social elevation as a result of South Sea profits – Blunt himself was made a baronet.

Hogarth hints at the true situation of the (non-stockjobbing) poor in the figure of the dying woman ('Trade') sprawling on the ground in the right foreground of the picture. Her condition signifies the deprivation of the labouring masses resulting from the suspension of real trade as the moneyed class invested in paper wealth rather than in manufactured goods. It is true that the ideas of John Law, which inspired Blunt and his colleagues, were in theory sensible, motivated by a desire to stimulate manufacture and commerce. His thesis, expressed with seductive simplicity in his book *Money and Trade Considered*, (reissued in 1720 no doubt to boost stock prices), explained the importance of the means of the money supply and the free circulation of that money to economic growth. More money would mean more purchasing power which would lead to more demand; more demand would stimulate industry to supply and profit from that demand, the result being an increase in the value of trade and therefore an increase in the country's wealth. The trouble was that in practice capital merely increased capital artificially, with little effect on real industry; resulting in inflation, which was inevitable when the money supply outstripped the capacity to produce goods.[20] According to the satirists an excess of paper money was chasing a few luxury goods. Pope, in a footnote to his *Epistle to Bathurst* complains that 'in the extravagance and luxury of the South-Sea year, the price of a haunch of Venison, was from three to five pounds'. In *The Broken Stock-Jobbers: or Work for the Bailiffs* (London, 1720, p. 16) one of the characters complains of the successful stockjobbers buying up everything with their newly gained money; they have so 'engros'd every Thing that was nice for their own Pallates' that he couldn't get venison to buy. The little industry that South Sea money stimulated was indeed in the production of social limited luxury goods of a narrow range, as *The Original Weekly Journal* (9/7/1720) indicated:

> We are inform'd, that since the late hurly burly of Stock-Jobbing, there has appear'd in London 200 new Coaches and Chariots, besides as many more now on

the Stocks in the Coachmakers yards; about 4000 embroider'd Coats; about 3000 Gold Watches at the Wh...s and Wives; some few private Acts of Charity; and about 2000 broken tradesmen.

Whilst the *nouveaux riches* were spending their South Sea profits lavishly, the traditional poor were as usual struggling to keep body and soul together. The newspapers, whilst reporting on South Sea fortunes also carry reports of desperate weavers assaulting their superiors, tearing the printed calicos off their backs, and being transported to the colonies as a result.[21]

The true situation of the poor may also be seen, in Hogarth's print, in the whipping and breaking of the two men ('Honesty' and 'Honour') and the dismemberment of a third person ('Fortune'). In March and September 1720, some soldiers were stripped naked and publicly flogged in St James's Park and Hyde Park, perhaps beaten to death, for petty theft, and Hogarth may well be referring to the brutality of these two occasions which were noteworthy enough to have been reported in the newspapers.[22]. Hogarth's figure of 'Fortune' resembles a foot-soldier – Fortune's hair, the way it hangs and its knot, is shaped like a soldier's hat with its bobbled peak; even the blindfold resembles the fold at the base of such a headpiece (compare the footsoldiers in his *Masquerades and Operas*). Hogarth may be hinting at the men – soldiers of fortune – who shed their blood honourably and honestly in their country's service, and at their reward: their treatment introduces again the theme of the betrayal of the common people by their supposed stewards and superiors. There is a similar feeling in J.B.'s poem on the South Sea Bubble, in the depiction of the statesman who

Extols the Man, who for his Country's Good,
And in his Monarch's service spends his Blood
(*op.cit.*,p.6)

but who is himself corrupt, selfish, self-seeking.

(c) Sexual Corruption

Hogarth's prostitute on the merry-go-round and the ladies raffling for husbands are recognisable figures in South Sea satire dealing with the corruptive influence of the new wealth on sexual morality. It seemed a time when the distinctions between whores and ladies became blurred; when the prostitute was elevated to the condition of Ladyship and the Lady fell into the state of whoredom as the one won and the other lost in South Sea gambling. We find both types trading together in the Alley:

Our greatest Ladies hither come

And ply in Chariots daily,
Oft pawn their Jewels for a Sum
To venture in the Alley.
Young Harlots too from Drury Lane
Approach the Change in Coaches,
To fool away the Gold they gain
By their obscene Debauches.
(*B.M. Satires* No. 1611)

The giddiness of speculation was comparable to sexual excitement, hence the double meaning of Hogarth's merry-go-round,[23] the emblematic goat, the horses of the whirligig like grotesque phalluses, the atmosphere of sensual violence, (the man whipping 'Honour' has a mask over his crotch, Hogarth indicating the secret, seedy pleasure derived from flagellation), and the symbolic presence of the prostitute here and in much satire of the period. One Bubble card relates the rhythm of sex to that of the rise and fall of stock, in the words of a harlot who on hearing of the decline of stock prices complains that

What I gain in my good Calling
By rising things, I find I lose by falling.[24]

Allan Ramsay (in *The Rise and Fall of Stocks, 1720*) relates the spread of the disease of gambling to the spread of syphillis in telling how successful speculators

Grow rich in Fancy, treat their Whore,
Nor mind they were, or shall be poor,
Like little *Joves* they treat the Fair,
With Gowd frae Banks built in the Air,
For which their *Danaes* lift the Lap,
And compliment them with a Clap,
Which by aft jobbing grows a Pox,
Till Brigs of Noses fa' with Stocks.
(1.101f.)

If religious disorder was symbolised by the Jew/Christian togetherness, and social disorder by the fraternity of Lord and Beggar, then the motif of the unnatural marriage of Age and Youth conveyed the sense of sexual corruption. It was a traditional pictorial theme adapted to the South Sea period – it is found for example in the Queen of Clubs and 4 of Hearts Bubble cards (*Figures 7-8*), in J.B.'s poem,[25] as well as in the song *The Satyr's Comick Project For recovering A Young bankrupt Stockjobber* (1720), where a suicidal gambler is encouraged to mend his fortune by seducing and marrying an old maid for her money:

Lay Seige to her for a short Space,
Ne'er mind that she's wrinkled or grey;
Extoll her for Beauty and Grace,

Figure 7: South Sea Bubble Card

A Brisk Young Gentleman Attacks an Old
Rich Fusty Beldam for her South Sea Gold.
She pleads her Age, He Vows she's Young and Health
And Swears no Woman can be Old that's Wealthy.

Figure 8: South Sea Bubble Card

A Grave old Fellow very Rich in Stock,
Well known to be a Lover of the Smock,
Kisses the Buxome Mother, and soon a'ter,
By Vertue of South Sea, Defiles the Daughter.

Figure 2: William Hogarth:
The South Sea Scheme

And doubt not of gaining the Day.
In Wedlock ye fairly may join,
And when of her Wealth ye are sure,
Make free with the old Woman's Coin,
And purchase a sprightly young W———.

In Hogarth's print the old women on the platform raffling for husbands, and the old hag riding the whirligig in the company of a young nobleman, reflect this theme.

(d) Mental Disorder

At the height of speculation, with Exchange Alley, as depicted in Hogarth's print, a frenzy of activity, it was easy for outside observers to look upon the whole scene as an utter madness. The newspapers tell of the 'vast Concourse of People'; Prior writes of 'the roaring of the waves, and the madness of the people'. The story of the Gaderene swine, demonically possessed, plunging headlong down a precipice, is evoked to convey the chaos and madness of the Alley. This tentative feeling of Satanic involvement – Defoe was to write that 'South-Sea was a general possession' – accounts for the presence of the Devil in Hogarth's picture, as well as in other prints of the time. Men like Law and Blunt seemed like Faustian figures, conjuring vast wealth, on a scale never seen before, out of nothing. Hence the images of the period, of alchemy and magic – Hogarth's caption mentions 'Monys magick power'. Toland described the accountant of the South Sea company as a 'Negromancer, Conjurer' and as 'Mephostophilus'.[26] Later, the atmosphere of superstition was to be surcharged by the outbreak of the Plague in France which coincided with the collapse of the Mississippi and the South Sea Schemes.

'I cannot understand the South Sea Mystery', Swift wrote to Ford in April 1720. The chaos was compounded by the fact that few people understood the mechanism behind the rise and fall of stock value. Not that they were meant to know; confusion was an important ingredient in the whole business of manipulating the market. Toland tells that Sir John Blunt was all for disarray: '"The more confusion the better; People must not know what they do which will make them the more eager to come into our measures"'. In addition the huge figures bandied about would have deepened the sense of unreality and madness.[27]

Inevitably, the metaphor of Babel was used to describe the chaotic environment, hence J.B.'s South Sea verse:

In *Babel* ne'er more different Tongues were heard,
Nor e'er more Nations in one Place appear'd:
From all the distant Regions of the Sun,
To this great Mart the num'rous Natives run.
(*op.cit.*, pp. 12-13)

It was an appropriate metaphor not only for the general folly and gradiosity of the Scheme but specifically for the breakdown of normal language, and hence recognisable human logic, and its replacement by queer business jargon. The whole of human intercourse turned on the question of money:

> If you resort to any publick Office, or place of Business, the whole Enquiry is, How are the Stocks? If you are at a Coffee-House, the only Conversation turns on the Stocks, even the Scandal of the Tea-Table is forgotten; if you Repair to a Tavern, the edifying Subject (especially to a Philosopher) is the South-Sea Company...even Poets commence Stock-Jobbers.[28]

Susanna Centlivre's play, A Bold Stroke for a Wife, first performed in 1718, revealed the nature of the new conversation. The talk is all of Bulls and Bears and Putts, of Bonds and Stocks, of Buyers and Sellers. The confusion is further increased by the presence of a foreigner whose strange, broken language perfectly symbolises the breakdown of logic:

> Wat Duyvels Niews is dat? 'Tis neit waer, Mynheer, – 'tis no true, Sir.
> Ik gelove't neit, Mynheer Freeman, ik sal ye dubbled houden, if you please.

The breakdown of the normal patterns and rhythms of civilized speech can be glimpsed too in a scene from Exchange Alley: Or, The Stock-Jobber turn'd Gentleman (1720). The setting, as in the episode from Centlivre's play, is Jonathan's Coffee House. A great crowd of people are present, , with several agitated brokers walking up and down crying out. Their language is stark, staccato:

1st Broker.	Ram's Bubble.
2nd Broker.	Bulls and Bears for To Morrow.
3rd Broker.	Noses Insur'd –
4th Broker.	Hempen Halters – who wants? –
Stock-Jobber.	What d'ye sell for?
4th Broker.	Twenty per Cent.
Stock-Jobber.	You ask too dear.

(p.23)

And so it goes on, with brokers crying out hoop petticoat or flying ship Bubbles, and bartering for prices. Then News Criers enter, running across the room in great haste, and tumbling over one another. They bawl out news from France, Spain, Italy; the speculation continues, affected by the content of the news. More News Criers appear and blurt out their despatches. The scene culminates in an expressionistic frenzy, in utter breathlessness and confusion. Such chaos at the height of South Sea speculation also typified the period after the collapse of the Company; the disintegration of logic and language in that period can be learnt from newspaper reports on the anger of investors and annuitants: at one meeting people 'broke out into Confusions and indecent Expressions', and only the threat of reading the proclamation against Riots dispersed them (*Daily Post*, 19/10/1720). In Hogarth's print the allusion to Babel is not only in the general confusion and cacophony but also specifically in the ladder upon which people mount the whirligig, the dizzy spinning of which will eventually topple them.

Not surprisingly, Bedlam and Bridewell frequently appear in South Sea satire. In Hogarth's print the seemingly barred windows of the houses in the background as well as the way all the buildings seem to close around the human beings, convey a feeling of confinement – the techniques here are those to be employed in later works like *A Harlot's Progress* (Plate I). Bedlam and Bridewell become general symbols of the shock administered to the national psyche, and the bankruptcy of the country following the collapse of the South Sea Scheme; they also indicated the actual fate of many individuals. The newspapers carry several items on the imprisonment, distraction or suicide of bankrupt speculators, men like Mr Walrond (*Daily Post*, 7/1/1721), once a rich Westindian merchant who lost his fortune, then his senses, and eventually his life; or Mr Allen (*The Original Weekly Journal*, 5/11/1720), a noted stock-jobber who cut his throat from ear to ear:

> They have dreamed out their dream
> And awakening have found nothing in their hands.[29]

Pope's dual sense of reality/unreality of the whole business is to be found too in Hogarth's print, in its tension between realism and emblem. There is a sense of actuality in the depiction of the scattered energy of the crowd and in the depiction of real-life people (John Gay and Alexander Pope are said to be present in the print), which is at the same time undermined by the emblematic, statuesque poses and gestures of these very people as well as by the presence of the ornamental figures of Gog and of the carved animals on the Monument. The emblematic features mean an abstraction away from life; they move the human activity onto a different plane in which it appears permanently fixed, consequently 'unreal'. The whirligig at the centre of the print is also at the centre of its meaning: it spins, but around a still point and along a fixed plane and circumference, thereby conveying the idea of the simultaneity of motion and stasis, of time and timelessness.[30]

(e) Economic Exploitation

The incident of pickpocketing in Hogarth's picture, as in other South Sea prints, is a microcosm of a society permeated by fraud and theft. On a literal level South Sea speculation gave a spurt to crime; the crowds in the Alley and the amount of money passing hands provided thieves with a situation ripe for exploitation, as the newspapers reveal:

> During the Hurry of Business at the South-Sea House, we hear that the Pickpockets have had a good Time on't; for on Saturday a Gentleman lost about 500 1. in Notes, and on Monday a Lady lost 5000 1. and they talk there of many other Transfers of the same Nature within this little while.
> (*Daily Post*, 23/6/1720)

It was only by such theft that the common people could share in the vast wealth of the period. On a symbolic level the motif of pickpocketing reflects upon the subtle craft of Directors and 'great men' who made rich pickings from speculation and stockjobbery. One satirical print, *Britannia Stript By a South Sea Director* (B.M Satires No. 1720) describes 'how a crafty vile Projector picks/Britannia's purse, by South Sea shams and tricks'. Such comparisons between common thief and South Sea director, forged in prints and in newspapers, are potentially significant to our understanding of Hogarth's later method (in *A Harlot's Progress* and elsewhere) of equating crime among the lower classes with corruption among their social superiors and political masters.

It seemed that men degraded themselves, descended to the level of beasts in the hustle for money, in the thieving and cheating and competition. Images of feeding or cannibalism recur in South Sea satire, in Swift's verse for instance, which was adapted and illustrated in one 1720 print, *The Bubblers Medley* (B.M. Satires No. 1610):

> As Fishes on each other prey
> The great ones swall'wing up the small
> So fares it in the Southern Sea
> But Whale Directors eat up all.
> ....
> Mean time secure on Garr'way Clifts
> A savage Race by Shipwrecks fed,
> Ly waiting for the foundered Skiffs
> And strip the Bodys of the Dead.[31]

Hence the motifs in Hogarth's print of the Devil feeding flesh to speculators, and of the man with hook and fishnet. The latter may be a specific reference to Richard Steele's project for fishpools (thereby complimenting the presence in Hogarth's print of the two other literary figures, Pope and Gay)[32], which was satirized by one Bubble card:

> How famous is the man that could contrive
> To serve this gluttonous town with fish alive.
> But now we're bubbled by his fishing pools,
> And as men catch fish, the fish catch fools.[33]

On the other hand it may be responding to the general piscatory metaphor of the time – images of fishhooks and fishnets abound in Bubble satire (*B.M. Satires* Nos. 1654, 1662, 1673, 1675 *etc.*). Hogarth also creates the suggestion of cannibalism by making one of the gamblers on the left (the Catholic Priest) resemble a turtle in his shell-like cape and bald head (turtles were delicacies at the time); the gambler will be eaten up or 'bitten' by his opponents. Cannibalism was a common metaphor applied in descriptions of gambling – Charles Cotton for instance in *The Compleat Gamester* (5th ed., London, 1725, p.8) described gamblers as 'Anthropophagi or Man-eaters'. Another Bubble card, satirizing a project for settling people in North America, depicts a group of Englishmen in 'Accadia', some gambling, others dismembering and eating a human body. In the middle ground a shark devours a drowning man, a lion attacks another; a group of native cannibal savages observe all this from a distance, no doubt biding their time. The Bubble card implies an equation between the cannibalism of these savages and of their bloody environment, and the economic cannibalism of the Directors who prey upon gullible subscribers, and to the cut-throat environment of Exchange Alley.[34]

The equation between the savage and the white man is found too in Ramsay's poem on the South Sea Bubble, with a different application. There the Indian is a victim not a predator. The exploitation of subscribers who purchase worthless stock from jobbers is compared to the exploitation of innocent 'natives' by merchants and traders:

> Thus Europeans Indians rifle,
> And give them for their Gowd some Trifle;
> As Deugs of Velvet, Chips of Christal,
> A Facon's Bell, or Baubie Whistle.

The presence of the 'savage' in South Sea satire is of course relevant, for the South Sea Company was granted the privilege of supplying Spanish colonies with African slaves – a privilege gained by Britian in the Treaty of Utrecht. In 1720 the Company's financial strength and source of revenue was in theory to be dependent on this slave trade. Although most speculators in South Sea stock through little or nothing upon the morality of the Company's commerce, others of course would have realized the exploitation involved, of Africans as well as of the American Indians whose land comprised the European colonies. J.B.'s satire on South Sea speculations mentions how

> Thousand swarthy Slaves do daily sweat,
> Beneath the precious Ingots pond'rous Weight
> (*op. cit.*, p.12)

and later refers to the 'mean abject Slave with dewy Brow'. In one Bubble card (*Figure 9*) a black boy conveying messages from a stock-

Figure 9: South Sea Bubble
Card

dealing Lady to her stock-dealing lover is an appropriate go-between: it is his servitude after all, the wealth derived from his labour, that sustains their sexual commerce.[35] Another Bubble card shows the black manufacturing snuff for the white man, and his suffering as the tobacco dust blinds his eye. Here again the defrauded and exploited subscriber to Bubbles is related to the condition of the black – the blindness of the former is compared to that of the latter and the overseer who works his blacks is compared to the Director who 'works' his subscribers into yielding up their money.[36] Finally the ragged, half-starved and crippled Indian pulling the Chariot of Bubbles in Picart's *A Monument Dedicated To Posterity In Commemmoration Of Ye Incredible Folly Transacted In The Year 1720* signifies, on one level the unstable financial foundation of these Bubbles, but can also be interpreted as an indication of the exploitation and destruction of native life that the European system of commerce involved. The theme of exploitation is again made clear in B.M. *Satires* No. 1659, a Bubble print showing Europeans threatening a group of Indians and coveting their gold. It may well be that Hogarth's sympathetic awareness of blacks (most powerfully expressed in *A Harlot's Progress* image of a black woman beating hemp in Bridewell) originated from seeing their condition of exploitation depicted in South Sea satire.[37].

2. The Lottery (1721)

Like the *South Sea Scheme*, Hogarth's *Lottery* (*Figure 10*) deals with the gambling spirit of the age. It lacks the cutting edge of the former print, Hogarth being more concerned with form than satirical content. Nevertheless its themes and motifs are recognisable in the context of South Sea satire. The enriching shower in the picture on the wall, the Cornucopia, wheel of fortune and turnstile, are all staple details in the Bubble prints. So too are the castle held up in the air by 'National Credit' and the windmill held up by 'Wantonness' – as Dorothy George says, 'Much is made of the imagery of the air' in Bubble prints.[38] The theme of perversion of religious values is communicated by the scene's echo of Raphael *Disputa* as well as by the detail on the right of the winner clutching moneybags to his breast in the darkness behind the curtain, which recalls the iconography in 'dark' paintings of a canopied Madonna and Child. Two further South Sea themes , of sexual corruption bred by money, and of an unreal environment, are present; the first in the detail of 'Good Luck' being tempted by 'Folly', 'Pleasure' and the Satyr, the second by the stage setting and its pantomimic features. Bubble prints frequently employed stage-settings (e.g. B.M. *Satires* Nos. 1631, 1653, 1659), speculators appearing on raised platforms like actors in a farce, with the presence of Harlequin reinforcing the sense of pantomine.

Figure 10: William Hogarth: The Lottery

'Folly' and Satyr were also prominent figures in Bubble prints (e.g. B.M. Satires Nos. 1612, 1620, 1622).

Finally there is in *The Lottery* a sense of confinement in the setting, of human feeling being totally regulated by material values – men have lost moral control over their lives and are being turned or tugged in various directions. The giddy turning of wheels – the lottery apparatus, the wheel of fortune and the turnstile – reflects upon this loss of human control. Spiritual values such as represented by 'Virtue', her palette and her books of Poetry, History and Divinity, have been neglected in the business of winning or losing money. The massive cases with their several locks that enclose the lottery drums at the end of each day's proceedings, also enclose the human mind. The solitary barred window through which is glimpsed a piece of sky adds to the mood of confinement. It is a detail Hogarth later employed so poignantly in the *Progresses* to contrast human imprisonment with lost freedoms.[39] The dark interior behind the barred grills of the lottery drums contrasts with this window and its sunlit view. Incarceration, madness and death are indicated by the collapsed and weeping woman, and by the two other losers who clutch their heads in despair; their gesture is counterpointed by that of the studious 'Virtue' whose hand at her head signifies the intellectual clarity they have lost. Other details like the dark, inward spreading shade cast by the curtains which also darken the edges of the scene, the collapsing floor and the sinister twirling and hanging of the curtain's rope further the sense of an incipient catastrophe.[40]

3. *Masquerades and Operas (1723/4)*

Hogarth's print, *Masquerades and Operas (Figure 11)* satirizes Englishmen's taste for foreign forms of entertainment, singling out Johann Heidegger (who appears at the window on the left), Isaac Faux (his signboard hanging near Heidegger) and Francesca Cuzzoni (she is the central figure in the showcloth hanging beside Faux's signboard) for criticism. Heidegger, a Swiss, was noted for organizing midnight masquerades in London, Faux was a famous magician, and Madame Cuzzoni, an Italian soprano greatly patronized by the English aristocracy. The vogue for Italianate pantomimes, as organised by John Rich (on the right of the print is advertised one such pantomime) also receives satiric attention.

In the 1720s, stockjobbery, operas, pantomimes and masquerades were attacked in one breath as being representative of what were most pernicious in English society. Leonard Welsted in a poem of 1721 for instance connects the South Sea mania of 1720 to the craze for Opera, masquerade balls and pantomimes:

> Wak'd from your dream, and from misfortunes new
> Less hurtful follies wisely you pursue;
> To low provincial Drolls, in crowds you run,
> By foreign modes and foreign nonsense won;
> To see French Tumblers three long hours you sit,
> And Criticks judge of capers in the Pit.[41]

Bishop Berkerley in an essay written in the wake of the South Sea disaster sees gambling and foreign entertainments as symptoms of

Figure 11: William Hogarth: *Masquerades and Operas*

the same disease:

> Our Gaming, our operas, our Maskerades, are, in spite of our Debts and Poverty, become the Wonder of our Neighbours ... The Plague dreadful as it is, is an Evil of short duration; Cities have often recovered and flourished after it; but when was it known that a People broken and corrupt by Luxury recovered themselves?

Jonathan Swift attributes the corruption of good sense and the decline of wit to 'politics, and South Sea, and party, and opera, and masquerades'.[42]

Hogarth's *Masquerades and Operas* appeared in 1723/4 at a time when the South Sea disaster was still a live public issue, as was foreign entertainments. At the same time as the newspapers of 1723/4 were reporting on the aftermath of the South Sea collapse, they were also drawing attention to the popularity of Faux's performances, to the rapture over Francesca Cuzzoni's singing, and to the great success of Rich's production of the pantomime *The Necromancer; or Harlequin Dr Faustus*. *The London Journal* of December 28th, 1723, carrying news of Robert Knight, the ex-cashier of the South Sea Company whose escape from arrest had created such a scandal and charges over the 'screening' of criminals by 'Great Men', told too of John Rich's latest money-spinner:

> Never was any of the Play-Houses sooner fill'd than that of Lincoln's-Inn Fields was yesterday was Sev'night, at their first performing a new Dramatick Entertainment of Dancing, called, The Necromancer, or Harlequin Doctor Faustus. 'Tis said, they had not less that 260 1. in the House.

A mind like Hogarth's would have connected the folly of 1720 to that of 1723. The pantomime itself (which is referred to in Hogarth's print), with its scenes of conjuring and transformations would have recalled the Faustian metaphor applied to the South Sea Directors. Details in Hogarth's print, like the windmill, Harlequin, and the man suspended in the air performing his balancing feat, whilst relevant to the actual content of Rich's pantomime, may also be seen as residual motifs from the pictorial satires of 1720-21.[43] Even the fire-breathing dragon recalls the Monument. The selling of waste paper (the works of Congreve, Shakespeare *etcetera*) in the wheelbarrow refers back to the selling of waste paper (worthless South Sea stock) in 1720 – vendors pushing wheelbarrows containing worthless paper stock (or else halters for losers to hang themselves with) are common in Bubble prints, which also show pieces of waste paper drifting in the air or worthless stock being used as toilet paper (e.g. *B.M. Satires* Nos. 1639, 1649, 1650). Just as in 1720 a foreign idea had been imported to England and had destroyed English business (i.e. the Mississippi Scheme in France which inspired the South Sea Scheme), so now in 1723/4 foreign entertainments like Rich's pantomime were destroying the English stage – or so at least the accusations ran. For instance, in 1720 the author of *The Battle Of The Bubbles* describes how Englishmen 'ran Mad and Transfer'd all their Wealth and Substance to Foreigners and Strangers'. In 1723 such nationalistic sentiments were being directed against foreign entertainers – the *London Journal* (30/3/1723) is bitter about the reception of Madam Cuzzoni and the rejection of English-born talent ('Mrs Tofts was equal to her in every Respect; but she was not born in Italy').

We find too, in the newspapers published around the time of Hogarth's picture, articles on the South Sea Company juxtaposed with items on the vogue for Opera. *The Weekly Journal or Saturday Post* (5/1/1723) contains a detailed article on the South Sea Bubble, the expropriation of the Directors' estates and the ban on their holding of Public Offices, and the same issue informs the public of the arrival of Cuzzoni from Italy – she was greeted with great applause, 'as are usual at the Arrival of Foreigners', the paper adds caustically. *The London Journal* (2/3/1723) devotes several paragraphs to South Sea Company news including the business of ex-Director Mr Craggs' estate forfeited to the Trustees; it also reports on the demand for opera tickets in a way that inevitably recalls the gambling mania of the South Sea period:

> The New Opera Tickets are very high and like to continue so as long as Mrs Cotzani is so much admired. They are traded in at the other End of the Town, as much as Lottery Tickets are in Exchange Alley.[44]

The comparison here between Opera and Lottery tickets also reminds us of the fact that the Arts in the eighteenth century were organized as 'projects' or business ventures with subscriptions and dividend payments. That the Royal Academy of Music which produced the Operas of Handel and Bononcini and employed Italian singers like Cuzzoni, Senesino and Durastanti, was organized on the principles of a commercial scheme can be learnt from a comment in the *London Journal* (16/2/1723) which reports on the Royal Academy's Court of Directors paying out a 7% dividend:

> It is thought, that if this company goes on with the same Success as they have done for some Time past, of which there is no doubt, it will become considerable enough to be engrafted on some of our Corporations in the City.

The Weekly Journal or Saturday's Post of January 5th, 1723 tells of Faux's conjuring performance before Lord Townshend and several other persons of distinction, and of his expected performance before the King in a few days' time. A few weeks later the potential satire in the situation of Faux among the rulers of State is exploited by the same journal (9/2/1723) – Faux's ability to 'cheat', his 'Trick of raising Money by Legerdemain' as well as the difficulty of pinning him down, of knowing what he will do next, are compared to the wiles of the Politician. His 'trickery' or 'Mystery' befits that of a Great Man – his is 'a Method not to be seen into by the Vulgar'. Furthermore Faux is linked with John Law, the creator of the Mississippi scheme and the inspiration behind the South Sea Scheme. 'When he was last in France he [i.e. Faux] taught Mr John L[aw] this Art, and 'tis known that his Dexterity in it surprised and puzzled all the World'. The same article had earlier expressed wonder at the magic of Faux, his ability to change little bells and sticks into living creatures *etcetera*, saying that the famous Magicians of Antiquity, including Faustus, were outdone by him. The whole article with its general references to Faustian trickery and its specific mention of John Law inevitably invokes the memory of South Sea Directors who were themselves compared to 'every common Gang of Conjurers, all the Ambo-Dexter Men of Bartholomew Fair'.[45]

It is not surprising therefore that Hogarth's *Masquerades and Operas*, following closely from the *South Sea Scheme* and *The Lottery* should contain matter reminiscent of the South Sea environment and of the two previous works. It is, in terms of composition, based on the *South Sea Scheme:* the Opera House replaces the Guildhall of the latter; Gog (or Magog) and the Devil presiding over the throng of speculators are replaced by Heidegger beholding the crowds flocking to him; Lincoln's Inn Fields Theatre stands in place of the Monument, and Burlington Gate in place of St Paul's; the crowd in the *South Sea Scheme* that spent money on worthless projects is the same crowd that now wastes away money on new 'projects'. The link between *The Lottery* and *Masquerades and Operas* is seen in the detail of the fool and the Satyr who in the former print pull 'Good Luck' away from 'Fame' and in the latter print draw the masqueraders to Heidegger; in *The Lottery* a mask lies on the floor at the foot of 'Pleasure' and in the *South Sea Scheme* 'Villany' (whipping 'Honour') has a mask hanging from his waist. It is noticeable too that the curtain and rope painted on the Opera showcloth in *Masquerades and Operas* resemble those of *The Lottery* print.

There are also thematic links between these early works, in the depiction of social disorder for example. In *Masquerades and Operas* Hogarth conveys the blurring of social distinctions by making the crowd on the right dissolve into one dark, amorphous mass. His print shows Stars and Garters jostling with common folk in the haste to attend Rich's pantomime, as they did a few years earlier in Exchange Alley. The presence of Royal grenadiers guarding the entrances to Rich's theatre and Heidegger's ballroom hint as Royal patronage of the trivia that replaced serious drama on the English stage, since the soldiers were there to protect their Majesties' persons: the *Weekly Packet* of March 1721 tells of disturbances at Lincoln's Inn Field Theatre and of a Guard of Foot soldiers being placed there every night, as well as at the Opera House in Haymarket 'in regard that his Majesty and their Royal Highnesses do often Honour this latter place with his Presence'. Royalty patronizes follies as it did the 1720 folly – the King was Governor of the South Sea Company, the collapse of which proved embarassing to the Crown.Hogarth's grenadiers, in a print that refers back generally to the 1720 episode, may well be a safe and subtle way of reminding the spectator of such patronage.

The perversion of spiritual values, or the lack of them, can be seen in the detail on the showcloth of the three noblemen's adoration of the prima donna – they bring gifts of money to her – which is of course a parody of the iconography of Madonna and Magi. Just as Madam Cuzzoni is figured in a perverse religious way, so is Heidegger: his gesture to the crowd below resembles the attitude of

Christ blessing the world, in religious art, or the Pope's benediction from the balcony of the Vatican. Hogarth here associates things foreign (the Italian Cuzzoni, the Swiss Heidegger) with Papist images. The Papist stigma can be extended to Lord Burlington, with his taste for Italianate art (the building in the background is the façade of Burlington House), as well as to Faux, as Hogarth would have known from reading the newspapers – *The London Journal* of January 5th, 1723, reporting on Faux's successful performances adds mischievously that 'Friends of Rome' are approaching him with the intention of converting him to Catholicism; they offer to make him 'Miracle Worker General' in view of his magic and legerdemain. Cuzzoni, Heidegger and Faux then are the new idols of veneration, exciting fervid appreciation as the South Sea Directors, who were also creators of illusion and folly, once did. The idea of the lack of religious integrity can be seen finally in the mixture of antithetical types – a Bishop, Quaker, Turk and heathen Indian can be identified among the masqueraders in Hogarth's picture; South Sea satire had also conveyed the theme of spiritual corruption by showing a similar unholy alliance of Jew, Turk, Catholic, Quaker and others.

The depiction of sexual corruption invokes another South Sea theme. In *Masquerades and Operas* the Bishop's seductive gesture to his female companion (he puts his hand to her chin) recalls the alliance of whore and clergyman on the whirligig in the *South Sea Scheme*. The Devil (emblem of a South Sea Director) throwing meat (i.e the fantasy of fortune in the form of stock) to the crowd of speculators in the latter print, is replaced by Heidegger who feeds off the masqueraders by feeding their sexual expectations and fantasies. (We recall here Hogarth's *Masquerade Ticket*, 1727, and the indecent double meaning of the sign 'Supper Below'). The thematic relation to South Sea satire can also be found in Hogarth's attitude to Cuzzoni: the situation of men offering her money is not unlike that of a prostitute and her clients. The newspapers made the equation which is implicit in Hogarth's picture, in telling how Cuzzoni was 'greatly caress'd and admir'd' by the nobility, and of how 'The Gentry seem to have so high a taste of her fine Parts, that she is likely to be a great Gainer by them' (*London Journal*, 2/2/1723; 19/1/1723). Moreover the fact that another prime Madonna, namely Mother Needham (the bawd in *A Harlot's Progress* Plate 1) was frequently making news at the same time would not have escaped Hogarth's attention and assimilitive thought-processes.[46] Cuzzoni's accumulation of wealth and her rise in social status – 'She is already jump'd into a handsome Chariot, and an Equipage accordingly'[47] – recall the South Sea theme of whores being transformed into Ladies as a result of lucky speculations or from South Sea profits being lavished on her by successful gamblers.

Finally there is the South Sea idea of mental disorder, indicated by the figure of 'Folly' at the head of the masqueraders, by the agitation and incipient violence of the theatre-goers, and by the man in the middle who scratches his head, bewildered by the nature of the modern entertainments, too full of common sense to appreciate the nonsensical happenings around him. He is a country type, as his rustic necktie and staff indicate, and he adds a Juvenalian aspect (country innocence vs city sophistication) to the satire. Hogarth contrasts his common sense, which is that of the ordinary Englishman, with the intellectual pretentiousness of the aristocrat and connoisseur who patronize Italianate Opera, Italianate Architecture and Italianate Drama (Harlequin, Columbine, Punchinello and the rest were of course figures from Italian Comedy); the country man's presence again introduces in a tentative way what was to be a major feature of Hogarth's later works (like *A Harlot's Progress*), namely its sympathy and regard for the plebian types, the social nobodies. Hogarth draws the countryman in direct counterpoint to the city aristocrat with his intellectual affectation – the latter aristocrat responds with a gesture of understanding to his genteel companion who points admiringly to the statue of William Kent,[48] whereas the former is simply and honestly puzzled by the idiotic Harlequin who is pointed out to him by his country colleague; the solid, clumsy flat-footedness of the countryman further tells of his down-to-earth mentality, whereas the delicately poised and raised feet of the aristocrat indicate the airiness of his ideas. Hogarth debases the fashionable William Kent (and the 'civilized' tastes he represented) by relating him to Harlequin – they are both dressed up in Italianate costume, they are both being pointed at, and from their positions of eminence they both gesture with their left hands. Hogarth is showing high Italianate art and low Italianate comedy to be identical in terms of their ridiculousness, and in terms of the money such twin follies attract. Furthermore, he insults Kent by making Kent's paintbrush, like Harlequin's hand, point in the direction of the theatre sign, as if to suggest that Kent's art, beneath its aesthetic gloss, is in reality no better than the signpainter's. Hogarth had a high regard for the popular art of plebian signpainters, an art which like his own 'modern moral paintings' were scorned by the aristocrats and connoisseurs. Philip Dawes, one of his assistants, tells of Hogarth's delight in the 1750s, in contemplating those specimens of genius emanating from a school which (as he would emphatically observe) was 'truly English', and how he would compare those painted signs and prefer them 'to the more expensive productions of those Genuises whom he used to term the *Black Masters'*.[49] Later, in 1762, he was to help in organizing an exhibition of sign-paintings, complete with catalogue, to parody the connoisseurs and their aristocratic art. We find these sympathies and attitudes prefigured in *Masquerades and Operas* in the comparison between Kent and the signpainter. Hogarth's final contempt for the fashionable Kent is expressed in his spelling of his name as 'KNT'.

Figure 12: William
Hogarth: *Royalty,*
Episcopacy
and Law

4. *Royalty, Episcopacy, and Law (1724)*

This print (*Figure 12*), with its presentation of the corruptive,
depersonalizing power of money, its bitter satire on the leaders of the
nation and their exclusive involvement in High Finance, is an
inevitable production of the years following the South Sea scheme,
the collapse of which had focussed people's minds on the nature of
political power and on those who wielded that power. Revelations
about the dealings of South Sea Directors and rumours about the
acceptance of bribes by political and even Royal personages created

an awareness of the sordid, grasping materialism of the rulers of state. Hogarth's print is concerned with the reality underneath the façade of stewardship and respectability. It is as if he is focussing on the idealized and allegorical scenes of Royalty, Religion and Law painted on distant ceilings – of the Royal Naval Hospital in Greenwich or of Hampton Court Palace – the closer inspection facilitated by the telescope revealing a sordid reality.[50] The Judge's face is a hammer, symbolizing his ruthless, crushing power over the common people. His role in City affairs is indicated by the dagger (from the Coat of Arms of London) which supports the hat worn by the Marshall of the City in the Lord Mayor's procession: the Law exists to protect the interests of the City businessman, to shield him from investigation and prosecution, whereas the minor criminality of the common people is not spared; it is a theme which was to reappear profoundly in *A Harlot's Progress*.

The King's orb is a bubble and his chain a string of bubbles. Hogarth may be hinting here at George I's involvement in the South Sea Company not only as its Governor, but also as receiver of bribes from its Directors. Knight, the Company's cashier, had fled to France with an account book in which he was supposed to have listed such embarrassing transactions; the newspapers reporting on his arrest in Antwerp tell that he 'offered to make very great Discoveries if his Life may be spared when he is brought over' (*Daily Journal*, 24/4/1721), which may account for the secret efforts made by people in Britain to prevent his extradition and which may also account for his eventual escape from prison. In Hogarth's picture the King's retainers and protectors are firescreens resembling shields, an obvious reference to the South Sea affair, to the screening and shielding of great men from scandal and prosecution.[51] The fire-screen metaphor was repeatedly employed in satirizing such cover-up operations, as can be learnt from the newspapers:

Yesterday the celebrated Skreen, so much talk'd of in the Town, was used for a Gentleman at Westminster, who notwithstanding his extraordinary thick Skin, and the Power of the Machine, was most dreadfully scorched.
(*Daily Journal*, 11/3/1721)

The large zero found on the covering of the throne recalls the multiple zeroes inscribed, *inter alia*, on moneybags in the Bubble prints, which signified both the vast sums dealt with and the insubstantiality of the paper wealth. The idea of insubstantiality is present too in the clouds upon which the whole platform rests, details whose hark back to the Bubble prints' motifs of buildings, castles, palaces and miscellaneous objects floating in the sky.

The depiction of the Anglican Bishop also recalls South Sea satire. His cloven feet hark back to the details of devils in the earlier prints. He rests his elbow on a pillar, (perhaps an echo of the Monument), which is juxtaposed with the trunk into which pours a shower of coins – all motifs familiar from Bubble prints. The point being made again is that the Church is not supported by the religious principles symbolised by the Monument but is in reality propped up by piles of money. The church-tower structure of the mill that churns out coins tells that the church has become a Mint. The Bishop's face is a Jew's harp connected to the Bible by a rope, the Jew/Christian alliance, as in the *South Sea Scheme*, signifying religious corruption.

Finally the whole business of telescope and moon, though a common satirical technique (Samuel Butler's *The Elephant in the Moon* for instance) looks back more recently to South Sea satire (e.g. *B.M. Satires* Nos. 1620, 1630 *etc.*) which employed spectacles and telescopes as emblems of the distorted, overblown vision, the confusion between appearance and reality, that typified the period of speculation. In Paul Chamberlen's *News from Hell: or, a Match for the Directors* (London, 1721) is one character who is positive that the South Sea disaster is

> to be ascribed to a Confederacy between the D[irecto]rs and the Fraternity of the Spectacle-Makers; to convince me of this Assertion, he drew a Glass out of his Pocket, and throwing a Guinea upon the Table, he bid me look thro' it by the Delusion of which it was immediately multiplied into Twenty. He added that the Hint was taken from what one of the D[irecto]rs used to practice in his own Family, it being his constant way, when he went to Dinner, to put on a Pair of Spectacles of Magnifying Glass, to delude his Appetite, as if the Quantity he ate was the more for seeming larger.
> (p.V)

Chamberlen's poem is dedicated to the Emperor of the Moon since the moon and its changing periods are analogous to the instability, the sudden shifts, in South Sea fortunes: 'The Sea, as all Philosophers allow, is your Favourite Element; and its Ebbings and Flowings, to which our late Vicissitudes are entirely owing, generally quadrate with your Changes', Chamberlen says in his Dedication to the Emperor of the Moon. The Moon is therefore the 'grand Director' of the South Sea affair, the fickleness, lunacy and instability of its inhabitants similar to those of the earth's (*ibid.*, pp. III, V). The moon, which appears, in crescent shape, on the top of the King's orb and sceptre in Hogarth's print, and in Bubble prints, (e.g. *B.M. Satires* No. 1627, No. 1649) features in many other pieces of South Sea satirical literature – in *Exchange Alley or the Stock Jobber Turn'd Gentleman (op.cit)* there is a scheme for the 'Insurance of Ships to the Spacious World of the Moon'; journalists send reports from the island of 'Dela-Luna', in *The Original Weekly Journal* (April 2 & 30, 1720; June 4 & 25, 1720).

5. *The Mystery of Masonry brought to Light by the Gormogons (1724)*

Lindsay summarises Hogarth's perceptions about the materialism of his age by stating that by 1724/25 he had

> already arrived at a mature judgement of his world. The cash nexus was driving out all other relationships; money with its 'magic power' had bewitched people. No one was content with his 'natural self' but wanted to assume a character more imposing, fashionable, glamorous. Life was one long masquerade of lies, falsities, pretences... The common folk were the victims of the upper classes, who set the tone and moral values; they were fooled by a Church that had sold out and become the tool of power and greed; they were ruthlessly held in their place by the state and its law.
> (*op.cit.*, p.31)

Lindsay's points can be borne out by reference to the recurrence of South Sea themes and motifs throughout Hogarth's work. The major series deal with money as a catalyst of social change – the Lady becoming a whore, the whore becoming a Lady, the apprentice and the merchant's daughter becoming aristocrats – and a catalyst of mental, sexual and religious corruption. In fact it can be argued that the South Sea episode with its sudden inversion or disjunction of traditional norms (the world turned upside down) gave a historical impetus to Hogarth's satirical method, the shock effect of which derives, fundamentally, from the distorting of conventional and customary data. In such satire (as in *A Harlot's Progress* for instance) the Magistrate becomes the criminal; the Doctor, by his quackery, a killer; the Bishop, a 'biter' and servant of Mammon; whereas the honesty, goodness, even holiness of the common thief or prostitute are brought out. In his *Analysis of Beauty* he gives a few slight, comic examples of 'improprieties' or 'incompatibilities' – a child wearing a man's wig and hat, or a monkey wearing a gentleman's coat. The tragic and bitter aspects of those types of inconsistencies however are to be found, for example, in *A Harlot's Progress*, in the dressing up of the low-bred harlot (Plate 2) and her presence in prison, still in all her aristocratic finery, among ragged fellow inmates (Plate 4); nor is there, in the *South Sea Scheme*, much comedy attached to the figure of the ape with his gentleman's sword – the ape's splendour, funded by South Sea profits, contrasts with the nakedness of the man being flogged.

Consistent too is the compassion for the people without money, the victims of exploitation, oppression and neglect, a compassion already present in the *South Sea Scheme* in the detail of the tortured men. Hogarth was later to describe such men, exploited by their superiors as 'patriots who, let what party will prevail, can be no gainer yet spend their Blood and time, which is their fortunes, for what they think is Right – a glass of gin perhaps to [raise] sperits and resolution ever to die in the cause, which often happens in these contentions. What did the greatest Roman Patriots more?'[52] The collapsed and dying beggarwoman in a later work like *The Times Plate I* (1762) refers back to the similar figure in the earlier *South Sea Scheme*: both symbolise the condition of the poor, their neglect by the moneyed class (*Figures 13-14*). That the poor were not a mere stick

Figure 13: William Hogarth: *The Times Plate 1* (detail)

Figure 14: William Hogarth: *The South Sea Scheme* (detail)

with which to beat the upper class can be seen in Hogarth's personal involvement in charitable causes, or in his giving of money to penniless, abandoned, half-starved sailors.[53] His regard for the simple wisdom of the common man, already noted in *Masquerades and Operas*, recurs for example in *The Mystery of Masonry Brought to Light by the Gormogons* (1724) where a plebian butcher and a Sancho Panza type see through and laugh at the pretentiousness and mumbojumbo of their social superiors (*Figure 15*). Hogarth's satire perhaps extends beyond the initial subject-matter, into the realm of political satire, for Orientalism was widely used for similar purposes elsewhere: in the *Weekly Journal or Saturday's Post* (26/1/1723) for instance is an article

Figure 15: William Hogarth: *The Mystery of Masonry*

satirizing Masquerades and Operas (Madam Cuzzoni and Madam Durastanti are mentioned), but with political overtones. The journalist has a vision of a pavilion with many rooms, in each of which various entertainments and activities take place. One chamber contains 'Cardinals and Chinese Priests, jumbling certain Ceremonies of their Religion together' and falsifying documents and parchments to make them support their beliefs. In another room is a group of

> Oriental Statesmen, that have undone their Countries by pernicious Counsels, and Schemes of Extortions. But they wear a Disguise of Honesty, thinking to make themselves popular; and have their Arms swathed down close to their Bodies, like Aegyptian Mummies, to avoid the very possibility of taking Bribes. These Gentlemen were never known to do a Courtesie, but for an Over-Balance of Profit, but they have often avoided the direct Odium of accepting large Premiums, by having the Purchase of their Favour come thro' the Conveyance of Valets and Courtezans.

The attacks on Masonry in the 1720s involved references to the South Sea as well as to the vogue for pantomimes, and Hogarth's print, *The Mystery of Masonry*, may have had these in mind especially following his own satires on the South Sea and on the taste for theatrical trivia. In the *Plain Dealer* (No. 51, 14/9/1724) which appeared two months before Hogarth's print, is an essay against certain corrupt Masonic practices, with two letters relating to the Gormogons attached. The attack on the credulity of coxcombs who flock to join Masonic lodges on hearing stories of witchcraft, magic, raising of the Devil *etcetera*, performed in lodges, is put in the wider context of the general credulity of the age, the gullibility of people who are 'so easily bubbled out of common Sense!' and 'bubbled out of [their] Sense and Coin' – the language here refers back to the South Sea period. The criticism of their gullibility is extended to their erstwhile patronage of pantomimes:

> What Staring, what Clapping, what Waste of Time and Money, did Harlequin and Faustus occasion last Winter? The Madness, both of Actors and Spectators, has often provok'd my Tears; I have even wept over the City![54]

In *The Free Masons; An Hudibrastick Poem* (London, 2nd ed., 1723), South Sea politicians and Freemasons are satirically equated:

> And I take it Court Politicians, and Free Masons are oftentimes ally'd; for it is possible the one may build Castles in the Air as well as the other: And whenever they enter upon Chimerical Projects, beyond their Accomplishing, they may be undoubtedly said to build such Castles...
> (p.5)

The anti-Masonic letter in the *Post Man* (7th-10th July, 1722) which specifically attacks the commingling of nobility and commoners in Lodges, uses language that is strongly evocative of the South Sea scandal:

> Abuses in a good Government are always dangerous, and to be guarded against; but never more than when they take shelter under the Protection of Great Men. The Guilty Persons seem by this to act as if they intended something extra ordinary, and wanted a Skreen from the Just resentment of the Law, like Tradesmen, who first get into the Service of Foreign Ministers, that they may be out of the reach of an Arrest, and then run in Debt with every Man that will trust them.

There are hints here of Walpole and the screening of South Sea directors, of the escape of the cashier Robert Knight, of the fact that men like Blunt and Knight (sons of a cobbler and a grocer respectively) rose to positions of social eminence under the friendship of the nobility of the land. The attacks here and elsewhere on social disorder, on the peculiar, secret jargon of freemasons, on the sexual debaucheries supposedly practised in lodges, on their atheism and their 'Hydro-pyro-geo-mancies' (*The Knight*, London 1723, by 'Quidom'), and the references to Babel as an early instance of the practice of Freemasonry (*The Free Masons; An Hudibrastick Poem, op.cit.*, p.8), would have evoked in Hogarth's mind the memory of the recent South Sea environment. Whilst some of his figures derive from Coypel's *Don Quixote Demolishing the Puppet Show* the overall composition of Hogarth's picture appears to be inspired by Bubble prints: one such (*B.M. Satires* No. 1662) depicts a procession of fools, with John Law, the subject of adoration, riding an ass which is being drawn by several hopeful speculators towards Quinquenpoix (the French equivalent of Exchange Alley); a crowd of men follow John Law and the ass. Sancho Panza is also present, and as the inscription of the Bubble print tells, Law and Don Quixote are identical. The procession of fools is a common emblem in Bubble prints: in *B.M. Satires* No. 1659, a satyr leads the procession, as he does in Hogarth's *Masquerades and Operas*. The procession in *The Mystery of Masonry* can obviously be related to those in South Sea pictures in terms of the similarity of follies. In Hogarth's print the dressed-up monkey reappears from his *South Sea Scheme*; there is too a hint of an earlier idea in the Semitic appearance of the bearded sages heading the Masonic procession (compare the bearded Jew in the *South Sea Scheme*), namely the idea of religious corruption. *The Free Masons, op.cit.*, had declared that Masons 'do Circumcision undergo/For Masonry's a Jewish Custom'. Jews, as well as Baptists, Dissenters, Catholics and so on, were in theory allowed to belong to the Grand Lodge, as the Constitution framed by Rev. James Anderson indicated: one of the ideals was to bring all religious sects and groupings together so that the Grand Lodge would be 'the Means of conciliating true Friendship among Persons that must have remain'd at a perpetual Distance'.[55] The Gormogons were thought to have Catholic and Jacobite leanings, as the *Daily Post* of the 3rd September, 1724 would have informed Hogarth: 'The Mandarin will shortly set out for Rome, having a Particular Commission to make a Present of this Antient order to His Holiness and it is believed the whole Sacred College of Cardinals will commence Gormogons'. In Hogarth's print Protestant Freemasons, Catholic Gormogons and Semitic-looking Chinese sages, one haloed like a Christian saint, commingle in a way that recalls the incongruous religious groupings in South Sea satire.

6. *Cunicularii, or The Wise Men of Godliman in Consultation (1726)*

Hogarth's *Cunicularii* (*Figure 16*) jibes at the false intellect of the upper classes – they are deceived by the false conceptions of Mrs Tofts, who

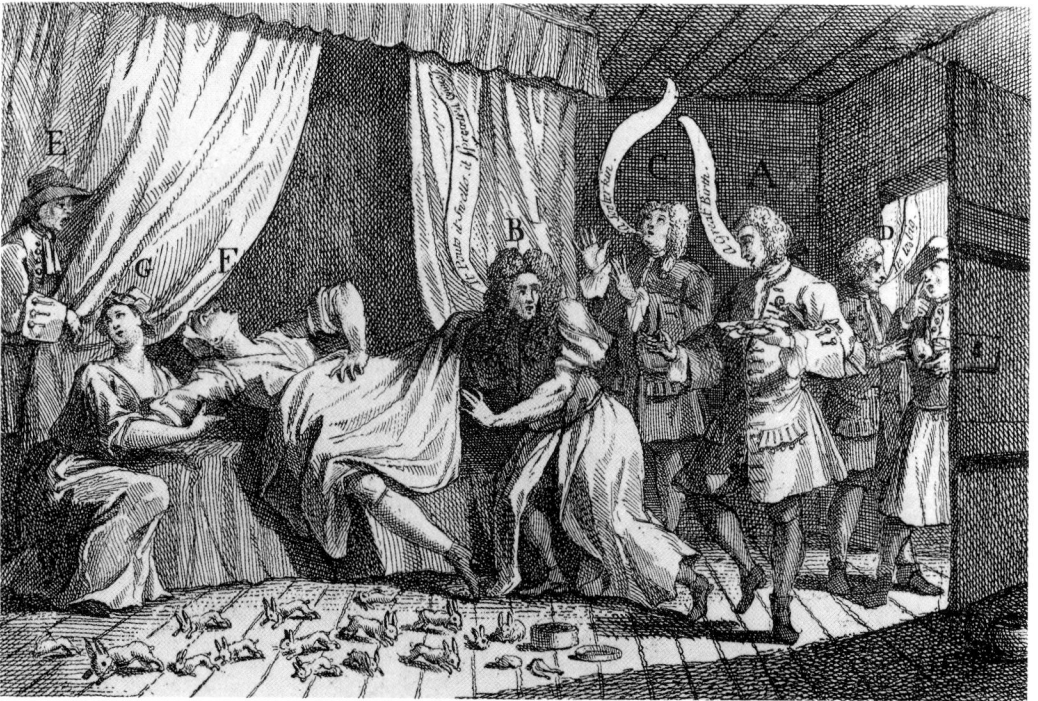

Figure 16: William Hogarth: *Cunicularii*

claimed to have given birth to rabbits, as they were earlier taken in by the South Sea directors and by the projectors who organized masquerades, operas and pantomimes. Defoe in his *Essay Upon Projects* (London, 1697) had used imagery of parturition to describe the fertile imagination of projectors, their 'Innumerable Conceptions which die in the bringing forth, and (like Abortions of the Brain) only come into the Air...' (p.4) The *Bubblers Mirrour: or Englands Folly (B.M. Satires* No. 1621) listed among the 'Innumerable Number [that] perished in ye Embrio', one scheme for 'Encouraging Wise Men to cast Nativities'. In *The Battle of the Bubbles* (London, 1720) the proliferation of projects in the South Sea period was described in terms of monstrous conceptions; Avaritia is the grotesque mother of the Bubble animals, 'a Dutch Woman, Famous for having Teem'd with many and most Ill-contriv'd Sooter-kins, and that long before she curs'd the World with the Infamous Litter whereof I now treat'. The reference to 'sooterkins' in Hogarth's picture, and the animal litter, perhaps look back to this earlier imagery. The depiction of the physicians as charlatans also recalls the recurring motif of the Quack Doctor in South Sea Satire (*B.M. Satires* No. 1650, *etc.*). Contemporary description of Mrs Tofts' fraud as 'legerdemain' (*Political State of Great Britian,* XXXII, 1726, p. 601) serves to further unite the two follies, and if Hogarth's memory needed jogging, then the *London Journal* of December 10th, 1726 would have done so; it reports on the Tofts rabbit wonder, and at the same time informs of the reputed discovery of the secret of perpetual motion:

> They write from Bern, that a Native of that place, an illiterate Man, and who, tho' a pretty good Mechanick, does not understand one Syllable of the Mathematicks, is said to have found out the perpetual Motion; the Machine is inclosed in a Box, and works continually, by one Wheel, which is affixed to the Side of it.

The project for discovering a 'Wheel for perpetual Motion' was one of the more absurd undertakings in 1720, seeking to attract one million pounds capital (*B.M. Satires* No. 1625, No. 1620). Mary Tofts too was an illiterate person (her illiteracy is mentioned in the tracts of the period)[56] attracting the wonder and admiration of the learned.

Her 'magic' which so entertained and excited the curiosity of the Nobility ('Great Numbers of the Nobility have been to see her', the *London Journal* of 3rd December 1726, reports), would have also recalled in Hogarth's mind the trickery of Faux, his 'magic' with mice, India birds and other animals, as well as the 'magical' transformations affected on stage by Harlequin's wand. Faux was still performing at this time since advertisements for his show appear in newspapers (e.g. *Daily Post,* 16/9/1726). Italian comedy, accompanied by 'Entertainments of Masquerades, Serrenades, Boxing, Singing and Dancing', was continuing to draw in Royalty and Nobility, as a notice in the *Daily Courant* (25/9/1726) tells: 'The Company of Italian Comedians seeing the Nobility continue to honour their performances with their Presence, are resolved to stay several years at London'. Such patronage was being satirized by the Press:

> On Wednesday last at the Opera-House in the Haymarket, was represented a Farce in the Italian language, by an Italian Company of Comedians newly arrived. The wise Men of Goatham gave it, as their Opinion, that it was very fine and extremely edifying; for scarce one of them understood a Word of the matter. (*Mist's Weekly Journal*, 1/10/1726)

Obviously nothing had changed since Hogarth's satire on masquerades and operas; the wise men of 'Goatham' and the wise men of Cunicularii belong to the same social class and share the same mentality. In Hogarth's picture, St André, the anatomist of the Royal Household, is shown with a fiddle under his arm and his stance indicative of a dancing man (the anonymous 1726/7 satires on the Tofts incident refer to his fiddling and dancing background, e.g. *Much Ado about Nothing*, p.15; *The Anatomist Dissected*, p.30), and his presence in Hogarth's picture automatically recalls Hogarth's previous satire on masquerades and operas. Hogarth depicts the incident of the rabbit delivery as a farce, like the farces and pantomimes on the Haymarket stage, picking up on contemporary descriptions of Mary Tofts and her associates as 'guilty Actors', 'Actors of this Fraud' (*Political State of Great Britain*, op.cit., p. 600).

7. References to the South Sea Bubble elsewhere in Hogarth's work

Hogarth's early pictures then, from the *South Sea Scheme* (1721) to *Cunicularii* (1726) have a logic when understood in the context of the South Sea disaster and the national moods created by that disaster. He was to refer periodically to the Bubble throughout his life. In the *Distrest Poet* engraving for instance (the third state, 1740, engraved after the painting of 1736) the map on the wall with its inscription, 'A View of the Gold Mines of Peru', amounts to (as Paulson observes) 'a memory of the South Sea Bubble's gold mines in Peru', Hogarth's reference 'underlining the poet's resemblance to those speculators who also pursued chimeras' (*Figure 17*). In 1720 it was the prospect of the South Sea Company's trade with Spanish America, including gold-rich Peru, which fired people's avaricious imagination. As Erleigh writes, 'maps, plans and pamphlets were specifically prepared to illustrate the marvels of the El Dorado of the South'.[57] The map pinned to the distressed poet's wall and the poem he writes, entitled 'Riches', are typical of the Bubble era's publications. The

Figure 17: William
Hogarth: *The Distrest Poet*

poem 'Riches' is comparable to the propaganda literature put out by desperate Bubble projectors who sought to attract the capital of investors and speculators.

The situation of Hogarth's poet perhaps looks back to the situation of 1720 when poets gained notoriety for their subservience to wealthy investors, speculators and South Sea directors. It was a time when Grub Street and Exchange Alley became one and the same avenue seemingly paved with gold. In 1720 Allan Ramsay wrote of the irrelevance of the 'traditional' poet and of the spiritual values and truths he traditionally represented, in the new South Sea world of money and sex:

Poor thoughtless Mortal, vain of airy Dreams,
Thy flying Horse, and bright Apollo's beams,
And *Helicon's* wersh Well thou ca's Divine,
Are naithing like a Mistress, Coach, and Wine.

William Bond, also in 1720 complains that the noble art of poetry had become 'the most Mechanick Trade' in the service of High Finance. Bond writes of

.............These Times,
When, on what Av'rice dictates, Folly rhimes;
When, Poets grown, who ne'er were Poets born,
Make Gods of Upstarts, whom a Mob would scorn;
To Miscreants sacrifice the Hero's Praise,
Prophane our Art, and violate the Bays.

Poets, Bond laments, have all 'turn'd Usurers of Sense', they have 'lent out Scraps of Brains for Heaps of Pence' –

When *Stocks* ran high, and Wit's Productions fell,
Wit grew a Stock, which *Wits* began to sell.[58]

The poet was a stock figure in South Sea satire, the airy or imaginary phenomena he dealt in being seen as analogous to the imaginary wealth (paper-stock wealth) that South Sea speculators dealt in. As John Gay put it:

No wonder, if we found some Poets there,
Who lived on Fancy, and can feed on Air;
No wonder, they were caught by South-Sea Schemes,
Who ne'er enjoy'd a Guinea, but in Dreams;
No wonder, they their Third Subscriptions sold,
For Millions of imaginary gold...[59]

Hogarth's mood in *The Distrest Poet* is comparable to the mood of Ramsay, Bond and Gay. His poet is caught up in the realities of a materialistic world and forced into subjection. His hopes of making money by his writings are as vain as the hopes of the needy projectors of 1720. He scratches his head in agitated despair, a gesture recalling those of desperate speculators in Bubble prints (*B.M. Satires* Nos. 1622, 1611, 1623 – the holding of heads, the tearing of hair) and of the losers in Hogarth's *Lottery*. The chimerical and disastrous nature of his scheme is symbolised by the set of mirrors hanging in the room above the mantlepiece, a contraption called a 'dare for larks' which, as Webster explains, was 'used to dazzle and lure these sweet-singing birds. Larks were an emblem of poets who were often called by this name in eighteenth century metaphor. The motif indicates that the poet is dazzled by the destructive lure of riches'.[60] The theme of delusion is suggested too by the detail of the dog at the doorway stealing a chop of mutton. In South Sea satire Aesop's story of the dog which had stolen a leg of mutton and subsequently, out of delusion and greed, lost it upon seeing its reflection in a pool, was extensively evoked to describe the delusion and greed of speculators:

> Gadzook, says he, here's Noble Luck!
> Here's Profit! here's Encrease of Stock!
> Here's Cent per Cent got in a trice!
> This Stock-Jobbing's a rare Device.
> He said – and at the Shadow snaps,
> And down the Leg of Mutton drops:
> Too late he finds what he has done,
> And sees at once his Dinner gone.[61]

Gin Lane (1751) may also be seen as looking back to the South Sea disaster of 1720 (Figure 18). Hogarth's picture of collapsing buildings, crowd confusion, madness, suicide and violent death resembles the scenes depicted in 1720 Bubble prints. Other details like the man and his wheelbarrow, the children plunging through the air to their deaths and the bellows that the man at the centre of the print holds to his head, recall South Sea imagery.[62] The snail on the ledge of the wall which is about to crawl up the back of the snoring man recalls the figure of 'Sloth' (a snail hangs from his coat) in Hogarth's earlier print The Lottery (there, 'Sloth' is the man on the left, underneath the curtain), and the church-steeple in the background with animals crawling about it looks back to the Monument and its animals in The South Sea Scheme. The new craze for gin-drinking is as disastrous as the South Sea craze in 1720. Industry suffers, hence the figure of 'Sloth' in both The Lottery and Gin Lane; The South Sea Scheme had also depicted the decay of industry, in the collapsed figure of 'Trade' (the woman on the right foreground). As with the South Sea episode only a few people profit from the Gin mania, for the majority are destroyed. If, in The South Sea Scheme, the church (St Paul's) was physically remote from the scene of human folly and misery (St Paul's dome and cross rise in the remote background), in Gin Lane the church steeple is also stolidly remote from the scene of human destruction: Hogarth once more is telling of the Church's betrayal of its moral duties.

That Hogarth, when depicting wealth, has recourse to South Sea imagery can be seen in the Four Times of the Day series (1738). Some of the figures there derive directly from Hogarth's South Sea Scheme – the frigid spinster with lappets flying, in Morning is to be found in the earlier print entering the house where raffling for husbands is taking place; so too is the earthy, pregnant woman with unfolded fan and one hand at her belly, in Evening (Figures 19-21). The Four Times of the Day series depict stark differences between the condition of the wealthy and the poor, and it is understandable for Hogarth to refer

Figure 18: William Hogarth: *Gin Lane*

back to his earlier works which also present such contrast: in the *South Sea Scheme* the poor woman collapsed on the ground in the right foreground can be viewed in opposition to the wealthy upright ladies on the balcony of the house; the same pattern of contrast is to be found in *Morning* with its stiffly upright, rich spinster and the crouching or collapsed beggarwomen.

Figure 19: William Hogarth: *The South Sea Scheme* (detail)

Figure 20: William Hogarth: *The Four Times of Day – Morning*

Figure 21: William
Hogarth: *The Four Times
of Day – Evening*

His final works, like his earliest productions, are a mixture of emblem and realism, or in the case of *Bathos,* pure emblem. They are again concerned with the world of politics and finance, and the crowd scenes, the hints of national madness, the satire on the Church's betrayal of the people, the reference to the National Debt, and the general air of pessimism and catastrophe look back to the earlier 1720s period. For example, a detail like the castle hanging in the air in *The Times Plate I* though meaningful in the immediate political context, nevertheless harks back to a common South Sea motif. *Bathos* is more evocative of South Sea satire, as if Hogarth is consciously rounding off his life's work by referring back to the beginning of his career (*Figure 22*). Its motif of Phaeton's disaster is probably derived from

Figure 22: William Hogarth: *Bathos*

Bubble prints, the Phaeton myth being a dominant metaphor in 1720.[63] Its general sense of catastrophe and details of sinking ship, hanged man, tobacco pipe and smoke, Father Time, collapsing building, empty purse and deed of bankruptcy, all evoke the atmosphere and the imagery of South Sea satire.[64] There is too the same concern for the state of the arts, the same bitterness over their neglect: in *The Lottery* is the reclining, collapsing figure of Virtue, with pillar, palette and paintbrush beside her; in *Bathos* is the collapsed figure of Father Time surrounded by objects including pillar, palette and broken broom (which is like a grotesque paintbrush). If in the *Allegory of Prince George* the three Graces willed Progress, Commerce and Civilization, and the hydra of discord was trampled underfoot, then in *Bathos* the three Fates are witnesses to a will made out to Chaos.[65] A final link can be seen in the re-employment of the Crucifixion story to convey the mood of apocalypse. The *South Sea Scheme* referred to the flagellation of Christ and the dicing for his clothes; in *Bathos* the collapsed posture of Father Time recalls the iconography of the Deposition, his crossed feet recalling the crucified feet of Christ. Both prints present a world without God, a world from which God has died.

Notes

1. W. Eden Hooper: *The Stock Exchange in the Year 1900* (London, 1900), p.2.

2. Cited by J. Carswell: *The South Sea Bubble* (London, 1960), pp. 113-14.

3. George Augustus Sala (*William Hogarth*, London 1866, p.95) wonders whether Hogarth ever held any stock of the many Bubble Companies of 1720. It is unlikely that he would have had enough money to gamble, and in any case he was firmly against gambling to the extent of not even playing cards (see John Ireland's *Hogarth Illustrated*, 3rd edition, London 1812, Vol.3, p.368.) The names of Kneller, Thornhill and Laroon are present in the existing South Sea subscription books, but not a minor, penniless and unknown artist like Hogarth. The subscription books that remain are mostly in the House of Lords Records Office: *Main Papers. Parchment Collection. Boxes 57, 58, 61 and 158.* Laroon and Kneller are to be found in James Craggs' list of the Third Subscription (*Box 158*); Thornhill, in *Box 57, Book 1*, which lists the names of investors in the First Money Subscription of 14th July, 1720, as well as in *Box 58, Book 2*, etc.

4. J.B. Nichols: *Anecdotes of William Hogarth, Written By Himself* (Facsimile reprint, London, 1970), pp.6-7.

5. To be fair to Harley it ought to be said that he was overwhelmed with similar proposals from needy and ambitious people. Swift tells of 'those thousands projectors and schematists, who are daily plying him their visions' (*The Correspondence Of Jonathan Swift*, 6 vols., Ed. F.E. Ball, London, 1910; Vol.1, p.280.)

6. Jarrett argues against Paulson's dating of this print as being after 1722, showing with convincing argument that it is likely that the print was made in 1720. (Derek Jarrett's *The Ingenious Mr Hogarth*, London, 1976, pp.58-59). See Appendix 1.

7. Cited by Viscount Erleigh: *The South Sea Bubble* (London, 1933), p.119.

8. The vendors of these pamphlets were whipped (*The Original Weekly Journal*, 30/4/1720). In Hogarth's *South Sea Scheme* the beating of 'Honesty' may echo this earlier occasion.

9. 'Tory and Whig...Promiscuous deal' as one poem tells – *The Yea and Nea Stock-Jobbers, Or The 'Change-Alley Quakers Anatomiz'd* (London, 1720), pp. 6-7.

10. The card is reproduced in J.R.S. Whiting: *A Handful Of History* (London, 1978), p.117.

11. *House of Lords Records Office:* Main Papers *op.cit.*, Box 158. *The Original Weekly Journal*, 27/8/1720, reports on the Bishop of Bangor being 'splendidly entertain'd at Dinner by the Directors of the South Sea Company in Broad Street'; *Applebee's Journal*, 6/8/1720, mentions that a clergyman was rewarded with 200 guineas upon presenting an ode to the South Sea Directors.

12. Viscount Erleigh, *op.cit.*, p.39,

13. Pope's *Epistle to Bathurst*, 1.135n., John Toland: 'The Secret History of the South Sea Scheme', in, *A Collection Of Several Pieces Of Mr John Toland* (London, 1726), Vol.1, p.443. Howard Erskine-Hill believes that Janssen, a South Sea Director, was the author of this piece, not Toland. *(The Social Milieu Of Alexander Pope*, New Haven, 1975, p.179, n.40).

14. *South-Sea; Or, The Biters Bit* (London, 1720), p.16. This bitter attitude can be contrasted to the earlier enthusiasm of Addison who marvels at the multi-national environment of the Royal Exchange *(Spectator* 69.)

15. Jews appear several times in 1720 Bubble cards (e.g. 7 and 8 of Hearts, 9 of Spades, in Pack No. 245 of the *Phillips Collection of Playing Cards*, Guildhall Library), as well as in Bubble prints (e.g. No.1611, No.1615, No.1648, No.1652, No.1675 etc. of *British Museum Catalogue of ... Political and Personal Satires*, London, 1873-83; hereafter referred to as *B.M. Satires).* In South Sea literature there is frequent mention of fraudulent Jews e.g. *The Broken Stock-Jobbers: Or Work for the Bailiffs* (London, 1720); Alderman Scrape, one of the chief characters in *South-Sea; or, The Biters Bit* (London, 1720), is 'an extortioning Jew'. This image of the Jew is of course widespread in 18th century literature – see M.F. Modder's *The Jew in the Literature of England* (Philadelphia, 1939) for the Jew in the works of Fielding, Defoe, Smollett and others.

16. *B.M. Satires* Nos.1632 (the ape dressed as a gentleman), 1620, 1636, 1642, 1646, 1647, 1654, 1660, 1675, 1684, etc.

17. *The Original Weekly Journal*, 2/7/1720. The same newspaper on 27/8/1720 mentions that 'Lord Castlemain's Porter hath got 4000 1. by South Sea Stock'; *South-Sea; Or, The Biters Bit, op.cit.*

18. To be found in T. D'Urfey's *Wit and Mirth: or, Pills to Purge Melancholy* (London, 1719 edition), Vol.III, p.63.

19. *A Familiar Epistle to Mr Mitchell*, cited in Thaddeus Seymour's *Literature And The South Sea Bubble* (Unpublished Ph.D. diss., Chapel Hill, 1955), p.115.

20. For the 'strange, unknown disease of inflation' which followed in the wake of stockjobbery, see Virginia Cowles: *The Great Swindle. The Story Of The South Sea Bubble* (London, 1960), p.81.

21. A special Act of Parliament was passed to restrain the violence of the weavers – *The Daily Post*, 8/6/1720, 11/6/1720; *The Original Weekly Journal*, 16/7/1720.

22. *The Weekly Journal*, 5/3/1720 and 3/9/1720; *Applebee's Original Weekly Journal* 3/9/1720; *The Original Weekly Journal*, 3/3/1720. See also P.G.M. Dickson's *The Financial Revolution in England* (London, 1967), p.156.

23. The whirligig is here an emblem of sexual giddiness, as in Richardson's *Clarissa* – see J. Lindsay, *op.cit.*, p.19.

24. 8 of Spades, reproduced in J.R.S. Whiting, *op.cit.*, p.171.

25. Pack No.245, *Phillips Collection, op.cit.*; J.B.'s *A Poem ... South Sea Stock, op.cit.*, p.22: an old woman purchases with South Sea money a 'needy fop to warm her frozen Side'.

26. *Daily Post*, 10/6/1720; for Prior see *The South Sea Bubble And The Numerous Fraudulent Projects To Which it Gave Rise in 1720* (London, 1825), p.5; for Gaderene swine, J.B.'s *A Poem ... South Sea Stock, op.cit.*, p.24; for Defoe, *A Tour through the Whole Island of Great Britain* (Penguin edition, 1978), p.111; for alchemy, magic and devils, *B.M. Satires* Nos. 1718, 1611, 1612, 1621, 1627 etc.; John Toland: *A Collection Of Several Pieces, op. cit.*, Vol.1, p.407.

27. *The Letters of Jonathan Swift to Charles Ford* (Ed. D.N. Smith, Oxford, 1935), p.85; John Toland, *op.cit.*, p.429; John Carswell, *op.cit.*, p.101, cites The Dutchess of Orleans' confusion over the huge figures bandied about in the Mississippi Bubble: 'Everybody speaks in millions. I don't understand it at all ...'

28. *Exchange Alley: Or, the Stock-Jobber turn'd Gentleman* (London, 1720), 'Preface'.

29. Alexander Pope, quoting *Psalms*, in a letter to Bishop Atterbury – cited by Viscount Erleigh, *op.cit.*, p.115.

30. The motion of objects and the implications of that motion was of course most interesting to Hogarth's mind. The basic principle of his 'line of Beauty' was after all probably inspired by a simple corkscrew in his mother's kitchen. For his use of a common jack to illustrate his theory of the

serpentine line see *The Analysis of Beauty* (Ed. J. Burke, Oxford, 1955), pp.43-4.

31. Eustace Budgell wrote of the Directors having 'drank ... *deep* Draughts of the Nation's Blood' (*A Letter To A Friend in the Country* , London, 1721, p.20).

32. The pickpocket and his victim in Hogarth's *South Sea Scheme* are said to be Gay and Pope – both were involved in South Sea speculation (see *B.M. Satires* No. 1722). The names of Prior, Pope, Gay, Arbuthnot and other literary figures are listed in the House of Lords Records Office's Subscription Lists.

33. 4 of Spades – cited in *Notes and Queries,* 1st Series, Vol.5, p.217.

34. *Phillips Collection,* Pack No.242 – 8 of Diamonds.

35. *Phillips Collection,* Pack No.245 – Jack of Hearts. In *South-Sea; or, The Biters Bit, op.cit.,* p.11, the successful speculator, dealing in stocks of a Company trading in Africans himself inevitably purchases an African with his profit: 'Mr. *Bubble-boy* (that half a Year ago was not worth a crack'd Groat) came down, with a Coach and Six Horses, and a Blackmore at his Tail'.

36. *Phillips Collection,* Pack No.242 – Queen of Hearts.

37. See D. Dabydeen: *Hogarth's Blacks* (Manchester, 1987)

38. Dorothy George: *English Political Caricature to 1792* (Oxford, 1959), p.74. For images of castles in the air in 1720 Bubble prints see *B.M. Satires* No.1620, No.1621, No.1671; for windmills. No.1620, No.1622, No.1646, No.1649, No.1650, No.1652, No.1660, No.1673, No.1691; for the cornucopia, No.1618, No.1620, No.1621, No.1624, No.1632, No.1652, No.1655, No.1656, No.1673; for Madam Fortune blindfolded and the Wheel of Fortune, No. 1620, No.1647, No.1672; for showers (of stock, coins etc.), No.1612, No.1629, No.1642, No.1647.

39. *A Harlot's Progress* Plate 1 – the piece of sky shut in by the buildings; Plate 3 – the open door; Plate 4 – the barred prison window; Plate 6 – the moonlit darkness through the window. *Rake's Progress,* Plates 7 and 8 – the barred prison windows through which the sunlight shines on Rakewell.

40. Compare the way the rope hangs from the curtain in Hogarth's *A Just View Of The British Stage* (1724).

41. 'A Prologue occasioned by the Revival of a Play of Shakespeare, written at the Decline of the South-Sea Scheme, 1721', in *The Works in Verse and Prose* (London, 1787), p.78. Welsted laments the fact that Italian opera has replaced English drama as the prevailing taste, that 'Shakespear to the soft Bercelli yield'; Hogarth too shows Shakespeare's plays being carted away to be sold as wastepaper whilst foreign entertainers rake in great sums of money.

42. Bishop Berkeley: *An Essay Towards preventing the Ruin of Great-Britain* (London, 1721), pp. 42-3, in *A Miscellany containing Several Tracts on Various Subjects By The Bishop of Cloyne* (London, 1752), *The Correspondence of Jonathan Swift, op.cit.,* Vol.3, p.116. Cf. the anonymous *All The Wonders of the World Out-Wondered* (London, 1722) which jumbles satire on South Sea with satire on opera singers and stage players; also *The Theatre* No.XX and No.XXI (March, 1720) which satirizes stockjobbing, South Sea gambling, and the taste for Italian opera and French comedy, as features of a corrupt English society. The author of *A Letter To The Patriots Of Change-Alley* (London, 1720) writes that South Sea has replaced the masquerade as the latest craze among people of fashion ('*Montezuma's* magnifick Robes, *Indamora's* feather'd Train, is no more regarded ... the Rise of Ten *per Cent.* charms more than all the Fiddles in Italy'), a point T.D'Urfey makes in a ballad of 1720 (*The Hubble Bubbles, A Ballad,* London 1720). For a final reference on the link between opera, pantomime and South Sea see *B.M. Satires* No.1611.

43 The way the man appears to be falling with his arms and hands before him protectively resembles the posture of speculators falling from the sky in Bubble prints e.g. *B.M. Satires* No.1621. Harlequin was a figure in Bubble Prints too as a stockjobber and symbol of folly – see *B.M. Satires* No.1648, No.1651, No.1660, No.1663, No.1678, No.1689.

44. For other examples of South Sea news and news about Cuzzoni or the Opera appearing side by side see *Daily Courant* 1723 (notice about the disposal of the libraries of ex-South Sea directors immediately followed by news of a new Opera, *Ermina,* at the Haymarket Opera House); also *London Journal,* 19/10/1723. For side by side notices of pantomimes and of sale of ex-Directors property see *Daily Courant,* 6/8/1723, 8/8/1723, etc.

45. *The Director Number II,* 7/10/1720. The fact that the 4th Money Subscription of South Sea stock opened at the same time as Bartholomew Fair began, encouraged such comparisons – See Carswell, *op.cit., p.174, 176.*

46. *London Journal,* 16/3/1723, 23/3/1723, 6/4/1723, 17/8/1723 *The Weekly Journal or Saturday's Post* 16/3/

1723.

47. *London Journal*, 19/1/1723

48. The three gentlemen are admiring the façade of Burlington House. Lord Burlington was a champion of Palladian architecture as well as a leading patron of Italian Opera (R. Paulson: *Hogarth's Graphic Works*, 2 Vols., New Haven, 1965, Vol.1, p.105). William Kent was, to Hogarth's mind, representative of painters who imitated the style of Italian old masters. Hogarth later called him a 'wretched dauber' (*Apology for Painters*, Ed. M. Kitson, Walpole Society, Vol.XL1, Oxford, 1968, p.87).

49. R. Paulson: *Hogarth. His Life, Art and Times* (2 Vols., New Haven, 1971), Vol.2, pp.335-7,345f.

50. R. Paulson, *ibid.*, Vol.1, p.128.

51. For Knight's escape, the scandal of it, and the employment of the screen motif see *B.M. Satires*, No.1712; also Dorothy George, *op.cit., p.78.*

52. Jarrett, *op. cit.*, p.190 applies this quotation to the *Election* Series, Plate 4, disputing Paulson's attribution of it to *The Times Plate 2*. Mabel Seymour (*A Group Of Hogarth's Later Prints*, Unpublished Ph.D. diss., Yale Univ., 1930, p.3) applies Hogarth's statement to the *England* and *France* prints (*The Invasion*) of 1756.

53. *Hogarth's Peregrination* (Ed. C. Mitchell, Oxford, 1952), pp.11-12

54. Cited in *Early Masonic Pamphlets* (Ed. D. Knoop, G.P Jones D. Homer, Manchester, 1945), p.68.

55 For Jewish involvement in Freemasonry see Jacob Katz's *Jews and Freemasons in Europe 1723-1939* (Cambridge Mass., 1970), p.16. Katz says Jews were not involved until the 1730s, but D. Knoop and G.P. Jones (*The Genesis Of Freemasonry*, Manchester, 1947, p.183) say that Jews were possibly admitted to Lodges many years befoe the debate on the propriety of admitting them started in 1732. See too J.M. Shaftesley's 'Jews in English Regular Freemasony, 1717-1860', in *The Jewish Historical Society of England . Transactions* (Sessions 1973-1975. Vol.XXV & Miscellanies Part X), p.150f.

56. E.g. *A Short Narrative Of an Extraordinary Delivery of Rabbits* (2nd ed., London, 1727), p.23.

57. R. Paulson: *Hogarth's Graphic Works, op.cit.,* Vol.1, p.176; Viscount Erleigh, *op.cit.*, pp.65-6.

58. Allan Ramsay: *Wealth, or the Woody: A Poem On The South-Sea* (2nd ed., London, 1720), p.22; 'Mr Stanhope' (i.e. W. Bond): *An Epistle To His Royal Highness The Prince of Wales; Occasion'd by the State of the Nation* (London, 1720), pp.1-2, 3.

59. *A Panegyrical Epistle To Mr Thomas Snow, Goldsmith* (London, 1721), p.2. For other poems that refer to poets and South Sea, see A. Ramsay's *Rise and Fall of Stocks*, 1720, 11.47-8, in *Poems* (Edinburgh, 1721), p.275f; Arundell's *The Directors, A Poem* (2nd ed., London, 1720), p.27; see too *Applebee's Journal* 6/4/1720.

60. Mary Webster: *Hogarth* (London, 1979), p.70. See too A. Dobson, *op.cit.,* p.64n,

61. *Several occasional and Humorous Bubble-Letters, Written to the Merry Journalists, In the Mad Year 1720* (London, 1722), p.28 ('The Dog and the Shadow'). For other examples of the allusion to Aesop's dog see *The Yea and Nay Stock-Jobbers* (London, 1720), pp.27-8; Allan Ramsay's *The Rise and Fall of Stocks, 1720*, 1.117, in *Poems* (Edinburgh, 1721), p.275f; *Cambro-Britannic Engineer ... To which are added Aesop's stockjobbing dog ...*(London, 1722).

62. For bellows in Bubble prints (an emblem of wind as well as of fire and destruction), see *B.M. Satires* No. 1622, No.1631 etc.

63. E.g. *B.M. Satires* No.1632, No.1649, No.1650 etc. for Phaeton. *B.M. Satires* No.1649, like Hogarth's *Bathos*, refers to the state of the arts in the Bubble era, and contains similar details – book, palette, globe and floundering ship.

64. *B.M. Satires* Nos.1614, 1649,1708 (sinking ships); *B.M. Satires* Nos. 1638, 1642, 1644, 1652, 1657, 1673, 1683 (tobacco symbolism and the idea of 'nothingness'); *B.M. Satires* Nos 1642, 1659, 1678, 1709 (Father Time); *B.M. Satires* Nos.1650, 1654, 1721 (motif of empty purse).

65. Their names are listed on the will lying beside Father Time.

A Harlot's Progress (1732)

1. References to the South Sea Bubble in Hogarth's two 'Progresses' of the 1730s

The South Sea episode scarred the public psyche for many decades to come; indeed as late as 1825 the disaster was being evoked as a caveat against new financial schemes and bubbles.[1] In the 1730s the newspapers were still carrying news about victims of the frauds (*Fog's Weekly Journal*, 17/1/1730), or else about the fate of one of the chief culprits: the trial of Sir John Blunt before the Court of Honour for illegally assuming the Coat of Arms of an ancient family for his own, and his eventual death in January 1733.[2] Nor had the Company managed to steer clear of further scandal during this time. The newspapers in 1731 tell of the dismissal of two principal clerks from the Company's Committee of Buying for accepting bribes from tradesmen (*Fog's Weekly Journal*, 27/3/1731). The next year brought a publicly aired charge about corruption within the Court of Directors and in 1735 Templeman, an ex-employee in the Secretary's office, published a scathing denunciation of the way the Company's supra-cargoes wasted money, falsified accounts and indulged in lucrative private deals with the Spanish, with the connivance of the Directors. Templeman starts off by recalling the 1720 disaster as a means of giving his indictment added impact. His book, which was widely discussed, dealt with financial frauds in the African slave trade, and is a culmination of previous charges made about the Company's exploitation of the Asiento contract.[3] Parliamentary Bills and Acts in the 1730s, some of which were concerned with sorting out problems derived from the 1720 period, helped to keep the South Sea disaster fresh in people's minds, as did private litigation involving Jewish ownership of South Sea stock (*Fog's Weekly Journal*, 6/6/1730).

There was too in the 1730s renewed discussion on the pernicious effects of stockjobbery, mostly resulting this time from the scandal of the Charitable Corporation's illegal activities. Thus Granville's stock-jobbing Jew as well as the stockjobbing characters in Susanna Centlivre's play were as topical as ever to the theatre-audiences of London.[4] Articles appeared in the journals expressing fears, identical with those voiced a full decade before, about financial fraud involving politicians, and about the decay of the moral fibre of the nation.[5] Sir John Blunt's essay in defence of himself and fellow South Sea directors was republished in 1732 as well as another tract sympathetic to the same directors, both presumably issued to counter the swell of public opinion against stockjobbery;[6] Parliament nevertheless passed an Act in 1733 designed to control such practices.

The South Sea catastrophe, as well as being kept alive by journals, miscellaneous essays and so forth, was also referred to in literary works long after 1720. Samuel Brunt's *Voyage to Cacklogallinia* (1727), a novel notable enough to be discussed in the newspapers (*Mist's Weekly Journal*, 15 and 22/7/1727), satirizes the materialism of the age by, among other things, reference to the South Sea Bubble. Pope, according to William Ayre, an early biographer, intended to write a major satire on the Bubble but left the field to hungrier hacks hunting for a theme. There are though several allusions to the South Sea episode scattered among his poems. Robert Knight, the absconding cashier, is mentioned in the *Dunciad* and the *Imitations of Horace* and the Directors are lashed in the *Epistle to Bathurst*. Seymour believes Pope's story of the rise and fall of Sir Balaam to be 'probably the best poetic satire of the South Sea Bubble' and has shown how passages from the *Epistle to Bathurst* echo satiric verses on 1720 Bubble prints. The South Sea is also a recurring factor in Swift's writing, from his Bubble poem of 1720 to the descriptions of the mad speculators and schemists of Laputa, in Book III of *Gulliver's Travels*.[7]

It is not surprising therefore that Hogarth's two *Progresses* of the 1730s, both dealing with money and its corruptive effects, should contain matter reminiscent of South Sea satire. This is evident from the prison scene (Plate 7) of *A Rake's Progress*, (*Figures 23-30*), in the detail of the scrolls falling from the pocket of one inmate, one of them marked 'Debts', the other, 'Being a New Scheme for paying ye Debts of ye Nation...' They constitute a memory of the South Sea Company, telling of the grand, lunatic schemes hatched by desperate debtors in 1720. Rakewell himself in his indigence has become a Projector or Bubbler, writing a play in the hope of attracting subscriptions and patronage. He is in this respect like the needy poet in Hogarth's *Distrest Poet*. Other details in the print like the prisoner with his furnace and crucible trying to make gold, look back to South Sea prints and their images of similarly futile alchemy. The telescope projecting through the barred windows, as well as the wings of Icarus on top of the bed, reinforce the allusion to South Sea – both telescope and Icarus's wings were commonplace details in Bubble prints.[8] Finally the verses accompanying the picture, describing the gambler

Figure 23: (above) William
Hogarth: *A Rake's*
Progress (detail)

Figure 24: (below) William
Hogarth: *A Rake's Progress* (detail)

Figure 25: (above) William
Hogarth: *A Rake's
Progress* (detail)

Figure 26: (below) William
Hogarth: *A Rake's
Progress* (detail)

Figure 27: (above) William
Hogarth: *A Rake's
Progress* (detail)

Figure 28: (below) William
Hogarth: *A Rake's
Progress* (detail)

Figure 29: (above) William
Hogarth: *A Rake's
Progress* (detail)

Figure 30: (below) William
Hogarth: *A Rake's
Progress* (detail)

In Seas of Sad Reflection lost,
From Horrors still to Horrors tost,
Reason the Vessel leaves to Steer
And Gives the Helm to mad Despair

echo the South Sea metaphor of wind-tossed and shipwrecked boats.[9] The previous scene of *A Rake's Progress,* (Plate 6), depicting a gambling den, is very reminiscent of stockjobbing scenes of the 1720 prints; the moneylender writing out a credit voucher to one gamester in Hogarth's picture recalls the figure of the broker transferring stock in the earlier Bubble prints: there is the same calm concentration and bespectacled attention to figures in the midst of frenzy and chaos (e.g. *B.M.Satires* No. 1672). Hogarth's reference to South Sea playing cards can be seen by comparing the 4 of Spades of one pack to Plate 6 (*Figure 31*). The card portrays a loser who upon hearing of the

Figure 31: Anon: *South Sea Bubble Card*

A Busy Fool, grown Rich by Empty Bubbles,
Pursues his folly till involv'd in Troubles;
Then, vexing at his Losses, grows Audacious,
Curses the Law, and damns each Scire Facias.

collapse of a bubble company falls to his knees, arms outstretched, cursing his fate. His head is bald, wig and hat lying on the floor. Hogarth's wigless rake is in a similar posture and in similar circumstances, just having lost a fortune. There is perhaps a veiled reference too to the involvement of Royalty in the South Sea gambling mania: a poster on the wall bears the Royal Arms and advertises the business of 'R Justian Card Maker to his Maj[esty]... royal Family'. The scene in Bedlam (Plate 8) completes the story of Rakewell's rise and fall, the trajectory of which recalls the South Sea story which began at the giddy height of successful speculation and ended in the dungeons of Bridewell and Bedlam. In Plate 8 the wall-drawings, of a ship, a crescent moon and a chain like a length of bubbles (*Figure 32*), and the reference to a crazy project for discovering longitude, all look

Figure 32: William
Hogarth: *A Rake's
Progress*
Plate 8 (detail)

back to South Sea satire, as does the presence of a mad astronomer with his 'Tube and Schemes'. The sprawling Rakewell resembles the dead Christ in religious iconography, so once again, as in Hogarth's *South Sea Scheme* the sense of disaster is conveyed in Crucifixion imagery. Earlier scenes in *A Rake's Progress* also echo South Sea situations, for example the marriage for money between the young rake and the old hag, in Plate 5. Plate 1 is especially worthy of attention in this respect, with its shower of coins, windmill-shaped arm of the smokejack that is tumbling through the air, starved cat perched on a treasure-trunk[10] and false conveyancing (the double inventory) of the cheating scrivener. The latter detail is intriguing when one recalls that scandal over the South Sea Directors' fraudulent accountancy did not end in 1720/21. In 1727 John Ward, who represented Hackney, was expelled from Parliament for forgery. Pope, who mentions him in the *Epistle to Bathurst* explains in a footnote to the poem that

> He was suspected of joining in a conveyance with Sir John Blunt, to secrete fifty thousand pounds of that Director's estate, forfeited to the South-Sea Company by Act of Parliament. The company recovered the fifty thousand pounds against Ward; but he set up prior conveyances of his real estate to his brother and son, and conceal'd all his personal [estate], which was computed to be one hundred and fifty thousand pounds: These conveyances being also set aside by a bill in Chancery, Ward was imprisoned ... During his confinement, his amusement was to give poison to dogs and cats, and see them expire by slower or quicker torments.

Plate 1's double inventory and cruelly-treated cat may well be a reference to this earlier event involving Ward and Blunt; Hogarth would have known of Pope's statement since it is likely that his story of miser and spendthrift son owed some inspiration to Pope's story of Cotta in the *Epistle to Bathurst*, published in 1733.[11] Indeed it is intriguing to speculate that it was Blunt's death that may have been the event that triggered off the idea for the *Rake's Progress* series. Old Rakewell dies in 1733 (Hogarth began the series in that year), which is the year in which Blunt expired. Like Blunt, Rakewell is a stockjobber – hence the India bonds lying on the floor; the miser's character resembles Blunt's in the simultaneity of his piety and avarice: he possesses a Bible but uses its leather to resole an old shoe. It was a well-known fact that Sir John Blunt was the son of a cobbler, and the shoe and Bible (Blunt, as noted before, was a notably religious man), as well as the box of old boots so prominent in the cupboard, may well have hitherto unsuspected connotations. Old Rakewell sends his son to Oxford and possesses a coat-of-arms; he is obviously a social upstart, as Blunt notably was, and the coat-of-arms may reflect on Blunt's much publicized trouble with the College of Arms in 1732/3. The reference to Oxford and, in view of the pregnant condition of the young lady, to the university's obvious lack of moral influence upon its students, perhaps look back to Nicholas Amhurst's *Terrae-Filius: Or, The Secret History Of The University of Oxford* (London, 1726), the frontispiece of which was engraved by Hogarth. The text satirised Oxford dons and students for their debauchery, profligacy and embezzlement of funds, comparing their ways to the deceitful stockjobber's. The foundation of the university is perceived in terms of the foundation of a Bubble company, the several colleges that spring up afterwards like the many Bubble companies formed in 1720 to cash in on the initial success of South Sea; the Chancellor and the Heads of Colleges are compared to the Governor and Directors of a Company and matriculation books to subscription books; a famous gamester and stockjobber is elected to the Chair of Divinity – familiar satire on the clergy and South Sea. Old Rakewell's decision to send his son to Oxford can be seen to be true to his stockjobbing character, in the context of Amhurst's book: there, the rush to send children to Oxford at its foundation is described in terms of the rush to Exchange Alley:

> Every old hunks and miser unhoarded his dear treasure upon this occasion, and thrust it into this fund, in expectation of vast dividends of learning and philosophy, which being novelties in those days, consequently bore a great price; scarce was there a country farmer, or a chimney-sweeper, that had rak'd a little money together, but must come into the fashion, and make one of his boys a parson, or a philosopher; nay, some sent whole colonies of male-heirs thither as fast as they could beget them, and were seiz'd with an insatiable avarice of letters and religion. (pp.60-1)

With regard to *A Harlot's Progress* (*Figures 33-38*), Paulson points out the connection between the clergyman in Plate I and his predecessors in the *South Sea Scheme* – '...like the clergymen in *The South Sea Scheme* he is oblivious to all else...' In the earlier print one clergyman, mounted on his hobbyhorse is being seduced by a harlot equipped with birch; in *A Harlot's Progress* Plate I, the clergyman on his horse, incipient harlot (her birch appears in Plate 3 by which time Moll has developed into a fully-fledged prostitute) and gesture of seduction reappear, albeit in a different configuration. The country maid with her basket containing a dead goose strangled at the neck also reappears from Bubble print imagery – one picture (*B.M.Satires* No. 1630) shows a country woman carrying a basket of dead geese, grasping the wrung neck of one of them and offering it to a successful speculator in return for some of the wealth in his wheelbarrow, in the way that Moll will trade her maidenhood for money to the point of self-destruction. Of course the goose was a common emblem of gullibility in British and European art, but it had become a particularly apt emblem in South Sea satire (e.g. *B.M.Satires* No. 1659). In Plate 2, the Jew and mistress situation, and the monkey and mask, recall South Sea satire. Rich Jewish brokers patronizing Christian ladies were common details in South Sea prints (e.g. *B.M.Satires*, No. 1611).

Figure 33: (above) William
Hogarth: *A Harlot's*
Progress (detail)

Figure 34: (below) William
Hogarth: *A Harlot's*
Progress (detail)

Figure 35: (above) William
Hogarth: *A Harlot's
Progress* (detail)

Figure 36: (below) William
Hogarth: *A Harlot's
Progress* (detail)

Figure 37: (above) William
Hogarth: *A Harlot's
Progress* (detail)

Figure 38: (below) William
Hogarth: *A Harlot's
Progress* (detail)

Hogarth's print invites economic jargon in its interpretation – the Jew is being 'bubbled' by Moll, he has bought 'bear-skin' (non-valuable stock) not bare skin, and the lover's secret exit and Moll's gesture urging departure amount to a pun on 'conveyance'. The environment of Hogarth's picture can be profitably compared to that of works like *The Ape-Gentle-Woman, Or The Character Of An Exchange Wench* (1675), published at the time when the practice of stockjobbery was beginning to be satirized, which sets prostitution in the world of speculative finance and commerce. It explains the whoring activities of milliners in the vicinity of the Royal College: the virgin apprentices are auctioned off by their Mistress to merchant customers who flock to her shop 'as to an *East-India* sale'. The prostitute is described in terms of fluctuating market prices: 'She'a a critical thing to deal in; having more Rises and Falls than Pepper or Indico's: She's one Commodity at several Rates'. The story is told of the country girl seduced and debauched by a merchant who then passes among male apprentices 'of whose company she is as fond as a Gamester of Bubble', defrauds them all, is discarded and eventually ends up growing old, smelly, diseased and homeless. In 1729 a picaresque novel, *The Life And Intrigues of the late Celebrated Mrs Mary Parrimore*, was published, dealing with similar matters in an updated way, using this time the South Sea Bubble as a backdrop to its tale. It narrates the history of a Hampshire country girl who ends up in London, setting up as a milliner opposite Garraway's Coffee House in Exchange Alley (Moll Hackabout's scissors and pin-cushion indicate a similar projected profession) where she does a booming sexual trade with stockjobbing Jews and other merchants, bubbling them out of their money by various 'schemes' and 'projects'. Growing enormously rich from her prostitution she takes a lease of a house called the Sword Blade Office (another memory of South Sea, the Sword Blade office being the bankers for the South Sea Company in 1720), and eventually 'tired with the Business, and like other great Traders, came to a Resolution to retire from this noisy Town, and spend the Winter of her Days in the Country'. Her progress is, as Richetti says, 'a perfect parody of the successful and righteous merchant'.[12] The deceiving of dandified Jewish merchants in the Royal Exchange by whores (Moses and Abraham, the two Jews here, like Hogarth's Jew 'aped the part of ... Beaux most ridiculously') is to be found too in another bawdy novel published soon after, *The Ramble, Or, A View of Several Amorous and Diverting Intrigues*. Extensive commercial language is used in this novel to describe sexual liaison between the whore and stockjobber – terms like 'conveyance', 'subscription', 'premium', 'proposal', 'bond', and 'arrears due'. *A Harlot's Progress* details of scheming whore and Jewish victim are firmly rooted in such picaresque literature.

The theme of social elevation and catastrophe also recalls South Sea satire which tell of 'Hackney Harlots'[13] like Moll Hackabout who purchase coaches from the profits of their business in Exchange Alley only to revert to beggary and Bedlam with the bursting of the Bubble. In *The Battle of The Bubbles* (1720), Oceana, a simple girl (a personification of the South Sea scheme) blooms into a beautiful creature courted by men (South Sea investors) with utmost industry and expense; she becomes costly, selling her charms at the dearest rates, in the end only the extremely affluent being able to afford her. The change in her status and condition is described in terms of a country maiden evolving into a splendid lady before ending up in the gutter:

> So, I have seen a tender Nymph from *Northampton*, fresh, and fair, and well-limb'd, and handsome, and young, on her first Appearance in Town, humbly content with moderate Gain and Shew; Callico, and Bread, and a Play, was an Holy-day Feast for Madam. But when the Heroes, at *Garaway's*, had once singled her out, and become Rivals and Bidders for her Love, and extol'd her Beauty, and enhaunc'd her Price, the sawcy Slut step'd out Dutchess all at once. Her primitive Lodgings, Up-stairs, grew worse to her than her Country Cottage; she must have a Parlour; a Drawing-Room; a Dressing-Room; ... a Berlin and Six, with a White Footman, and a Black Valet, was the least Attendance her Grace could be content with: Her Callico grew into a Damask; her Damask was metamorphos'd into a Brocade...' (p.13)

Eventually the gentry desert her when they discover that she has cuckolded them; 'she keeps Bullies; she Paints, she Patches, and Palmes false Dice upon them all at Play', and finally ends up in an old garret 'there to starve, die, and dissolve'. The outline of Moll Hackabout's progress is prefigured in the story of Oceana.

Needless to say the rise and decline of harlots is a tale that predates South Sea satire, but what the South Sea incident provided was a manifestly real, contemporary situation in which to attach the tale. A related traditional theme is of the contrast between country and city, and again South Sea created a fertile culture in which to seed the idea. On a superficial level there is indulgence in idyllic concepts, a nostalgia for simpler systems, for 'th'old-fashioned Ways' of rural living, hence the stories of Damons who sell their flocks, fling away their crooks, to journey to Exchange Alley, only to return disillusioned to their rural bowers.[14] In Berkeley's case however the response is deeper, the South Sea experience revealing to him the urgent need for moral regeneration, for new beginnings in new, unspoilt lands.[15]

A Harlot's Progress, with its country-city structure, needs to be understood in the climate of ideas and emotions created in the previous decade. Moll on entering the city is descended upon by vultures who will exploit her sexually and economically. The themes of sexual corruption and of economic cannibalism present in Hogarth's *South Sea Scheme* are reworked and expanded in his satirical series of 1732.

2. The South Sea Bubble compared with the Charitable Corporation frauds, and both linked to Walpole

Throughout the 1720s and 1730s, in prints, newspapers and literature, the South Sea fraud was employed as a keen weapon in the barrage of satire directed against Sir Robert Walpole and his Administration. The 'screen' metaphor, evolved in 1721, was still being applied to Walpole's name to the very end of his career, in prints that refers to his part in the handling of South Sea affairs.[16] Walpole, it was said, had drawn up an agreement between the faltering Company and the Bank of England whereby the former would gain access to the latter's capital; when the Bank's directors pulled out of the deal the shares of the South Sea company plummeted. The controversy over the Bank Contract was renewed in 1730/1 with Opposition innuendoes about shady dealings for private profit, until Walpole in 1735 was forced into undertaking to explain his part in the transaction.[17] The epithets of 'stockjobber' and 'projector' came to be attached to his name, especially in the furious diatribes against his Excise Scheme of 1733:

> Against the Sturdy Beggars
> The Grand Projector raves,
> For had they not oppos'd his Scheme
> We soon shou'd have been Slaves.[18]

He was frequently accused of using his office, his superior ministerial knowledge of political events, to anticipate and exploit the movement of stock and other securities, and as late as 1743 he was being compared to South Sea culprits, specifically to Robert Knight the ex-cashier of the Company.[19] Opposition newspapers attacked him for encouraging, by his own example, avarice in the heart of the nation: *The Craftsman* (17/5/1729) described how people are 'sunk in the Love of Wealth... Corruption has introduced luxury...and now the sole Government among them seems to be Money. By this Instrument the Ambitious rule'; *Mist's Weekly Journal* (22/1/1726) wrote of 'Money being the secret Spring which governs Mankind; especially in these Times'.

Disillusion with the corrupt and grossly materialistic climate of Walpolian England was deepened in the 1730s by a new national scandal which bore many of the hallmarks of the previous decade's South Sea fraud. In October 1731 news broke of the escape to France of John Thomson, the warehouse keeper of the Charitable Corporation, who took with him a great many valuables and jewels belonging to the depositors as well as the account books of the Corporation.[20] Thomson's action was profoundly shocking and it immediately became the latest sensation and talking point in Parliament and in coffee-houses. Earlier in the year the Lord Mayor and the Common Council of the City of London had been presented with a petition which outlined anxieties over the dealings of the proprietors of the Charitable Corporation. A month later, on March 13th and 15th, 1731, Parliament had received two separate petitions by the Sheriffs of London and City Merchants on the 'pernicious practices' of the Corporation, with a further two petitions from other bodies following. Now, with the absconding of Thomson, such accusations were to prove more substantial than even the petitioners could have believed.

The Charitable Corporation had received the Royal Charter in 1708 as a project which, like the South Sea scheme, appeared to be potentially beneficial to the public. The plan was to reduce the power of extortionate pawnbrokers by lending money to the poor upon recoverable pledges and at a charge of 5%. Subscribers to the scheme were to be reassured that their capital was not only accumulating interest but also working for the welfare of the poor. However at its very inception doubts were being raised as to the integrity and charitable claims of its directors: 'Certainly those Men of the Cha. Corp. whatever they style themselves, must have some other Ends beside Charity...'[21] The Corporation eventually departed from its charitable ideals, degenerating into a speculative business venture, with rich people using its funds. Sir Archibald Grant and other directors borrowed large sums upon fictitious pledges from the Corporation's capital to deal in York Building Company Stock. In 1732, Grant, Sutton, Robinson and Bond, all Members of Parliament and all involved in the affairs of the Corporation, were expelled from the House for their part in the fraud. Throughout the 1720s and in 1730 investigations into the abuse of various charitable trusts were being undertaken all over the country[22] – news of the Corporation's fraud served to deepen people's distress about the decay of Christian values, about corruption in high places at the expense of the poor and the common people. 'It is a method invented by some very wise men, by which the rich may be charitable to the poor and by money in pocket for it', says Stocks cynically of the Charitable Corporation, in Fielding's play *The Lottery* (1732).

This latest public fraud was immediately compared to the previous South Sea scandal in its destructive effects. 'Even by the fatal South-Sea Scheme, less Mischief was done in Proportion', one newspaper commented. Another wrote of 'a most unheard of Villany ever projected, even worse in proportion than the fatal South Sea Scheme'.[23] The stockjobbing, the involvement of Members of Parliament and of Jews, the impoverishment and suicide of some of the victims and the drift into prostitution of others, were some of the features that link South Sea and the Charitable Corporation:

The distress occasioned by this bankruptcy was appalling, pervading nearly every class of society... The small capitalist was entirely ruined...The poor were unable to get their goods; the rich were robbed of their jewels; families accustomed to affluence were starving; delicate women, hitherto irreproachable, were compelled to exchange their persons for bread...[24]

Walpole was again widely vilified by the Opposition press which linked him to the prime villains of the Corporations and which perceived its frauds as symbolic of the spirit of avarice and corruption presiding in his reign.

Hogarth in 1731 whilst working on *A Harlot's Progress* would have followed the Charitable Corporation scandal closely in view of his business acquaintance with its leading culprits. Two years previously a House of Commons Committee which included Sir Archibald Grant among its members had been appointed to enquire into prison conditions, and Hogarth had sketched th Committee's investigation of Bambridge's administration of the Fleet prison. Grant commissioned from Hogarth a copy of his oil painting of the Fleet proceedings, as well as a copy of Hogarth's *Beggar's Opera,* but Grant as a result of his demise in 1732 over his part in the Corporation fraud never collected or paid for the two paintings, Hogarth having to sell them instead to William Huggins. John Thomson, the absconding warehouse keeper, who was also on the same Commons Committee investigating the prisons had ordered two erotic paintings from Hogarth, *Before* and *After,*but never received or paid for them either, having fled to France with the Corporation's funds. As to Sutton, the other major Corporation villain, Hogarth may have known about him from his acquaintance with Oglethorpe in 1729, when Hogarth painted the prison enquiry Committee which was headed by Oglethorpe. Sutton was Oglethorpe's cousin and in 1732, when Parliament introduced the motion to expel Sutton, Oglethorpe was only one of two Members – the other being Sutton's brother – to vote against it.[25] Hogarth, always a keen, sometimes ruthless, businessman when it came to collecting money for commissions he had executed, would have had personal reasons for feeling some animosity towards the Charitable Corporation crooks. He may have even identified with the victims of the fraud for it had, indirectly, left him out of pocket at a time in his career when every pound he earned counted.

The South Sea frauds then, linked with those of the Charitable Corporation, proved a constant source of embarrassment to Walpole and mention of them in a satirical context was commonly a means of pointing to his corrupt administration. At the time of *A Harlot's Progress* the tendency of satire, verbal and pictorial, was overwhelmingly anti-Walpolian. Such satire 'grew by giant strides in the years following 1725... Between 1730 and 1731 Britain was deluged with anti-Walpole ballads and literature'. David Hume, in 1742, wrote that Walpole was 'the subject of above half the paper that has been blotted in the nation within these twenty years'.[26] One of the high points of such attacks on Walpole came with the production of Gay's *Beggar's Opera* in 1728, a play that Hogarth was most familiar with. The world of Gay's play is a squalidly commercial city of whore, pimp, thief, Jewish merchant and prison warder, a world in which 'Money well timed, and properly applied, will do anything', as Macheath declares (Act II, Scene 12). Gay constantly draws parallels between thieves and whores and their social superiors, the politicians, courtiers and company directors, and there are recurring references to the South Sea Bubble in his play (Act II, Scene 13, Air XVIII; Act III, Scene 3, Air II, etc.) As David Lindsay put it, 'we are left with a sense of the destructive force of those purely commercial values which Peachum shares with Sir Robert Walpole and the South Sea directors'.[27] *A Harlot's Progress* reflects much of the low-life atmosphere of Gay's play; it also points, albeit less obviously, to the world of politicians and their creatures, a fact that has so far escaped attention because critics have failed to obtain more biographical data on the main characters present in Hogarth's pictures, or have failed to appreciate that pictorial and literary satire in the 1730s was overwhelmingly directed against Walpole. The facts are these: that all the main types or characters present in or mentioned satirically in *A Harlot's Progress* (Colonel Charteris – Plate 1; Bishop Gibson – Plates 1 and 3; Thomas Woolston – Plate 2; the Jew – Plate 2; Sir John Gonson – Plate 3; the Prison Warder – Plate 4; the Quack – Plate 5) were connected to Walpole in various ways – either they were in his pay, or else their villainies were seen by contemporaries as being representative of Walpole's own immortality; or else, in the case of Thomas Woolston, the reference is to the opposition to Walpole's administration.

3. 'A Harlot's Progress' as political allegory

(a) Plate 1: Colonel Charteris and Sir Robert Walpole; Moll as Britannia (Figure 33)

A footnote in Paulson's massive biography of Hogarth is about all there has been written so far about *A Harlot's Progress* as anti-Walpole satire. 'Hogarth', Paulson writes, 'had, perhaps, opened the door to political innuendo in the *Harlot* by the introduction of Walpole's "friend" Charteris'.[28] The observation is nevertheless central in any consideration of the politics of Hogarth's series. One of the ways of attacking Walpole and (hopefully) circumventing the libel laws was by satirizing a villain, mythical or historical, ancient or modern, whose immorality was made to serve as an analogue to Walpole's. By the time of *A Harlot's Progress* this satirical convention was so firmly established and effective that, as one Grub-street production puts it, 'if the character of a ROGUE should be drawn in *Lapland*, and brought to our Town, *Bob* immediately starts up, and swears, it can mean no Body but himself'.[29] Colonel Charteris was one such rogue, described by Gay and others as a 'Great Man',[30] the epithet having obvious political connotation from its constant application by satirists to Walpole. Dr Arbuthnot's epitaph on Charteris signify the way Charteris was used to get at Walpole:

> Nor was he more singular
> in the undeviating *Pravity* of his *Manners*
>   Than successful
>   in *Accumulating* WEALTH
> For, without TRADE or PROFESSION,
>   Without TRUST of PUBLIC MONEY,
> And without BRIBE-WORTHY Service,
> He acquired, or more properly created,
>   A MINISTERIAL ESTATE.
> (*Epistle to Bathurst*, 1.20n)

The terminology as well as the similarity to satirical epitaphs on Cardinal Wolsey (an analogue of Walpole) in *The Craftsman*[31] point to the link between Charteris and Walpole. Nor was their relationship purely fictional: there were many accusations as to the friendship and complicity between them. One ballad of 1730 describing the Colonel as 'A Favourite Worthy of Bobby the Great' claims that Walpole had warned him of the danger of impending conviction for rape:

> Bob told him before-hand, to give him his due,
> Dear Col'nel, a Jury may make you look blue.

When Charteris was sentenced to death he applied to Walpole for aid:

> But when Verdict was past, he was down in the Dumps,
> And for Shifts and Excuses Sir *William* he pumps;
> Ay, and Bobby the *Screen* too was put to his Trumps,
> Which no body can deny[32]

The *Grub Street Journal* of September 10th, 1730 carries reports from several newspapers of Charteris presenting a lavish gift to Walpole.[33]

Charteris, apart from being a notorious rake was also an enormously wealthy man, astute and corrupt. His background was widely known from the facts presented in 1730 in journals and broadsheets, especially the scandal over his exploitation of debtors some twenty years previously. He had wrung large sums of money from bankrupts and distressed tradesmen in return for enlisting them in his company of foot-guards where they would be, according to the provisions of a recent act of Parliament relating to debtors, immune from prosecution. The debtors never actually served in Charteris' company – their names were merely added to the roster and he then pocketed the Government wages apparently due to them. Reading about such matters in 1730 would undoubtedly have evoked personal anger in Hogarth; as Paulson writes, he would have 'recalled bitter memories of twenty years earlier when his father was petitioning for release from debtors' prison and the Insolvency Bill was creeping along in the House of Commons'.[34] The recollection that Charteris, when questioned in Parliament in 1711, was then merely reprimanded by the Speaker for his crimes would have intensified Hogarth's disillusion with the political system administered by 'Great Men' and would have made Charteris appear even more symbolic of political corruption.

Charteris increased the store of money embezzled from the Government by gambling and usury, and he became a substantial landowner. In 1713 he bought up the extensive lands of the Newmills Cloth Manufactory in Scotland when the Company was wound up.[35] He also invested heavily in South Sea stock, his name appearing on the voting list for the year 1714 with no less that four stars beside it, indicating that he was qualified, by the size of his holding, to be elected Governor, Sub-Governor, Deputy Governor or as one of the Directors of the Company. In 1720 he was a major speculator, subscribing massive sums; in the case of the First Money Subscription of South Sea stock commenced on April 14th he invested £3,000, one of the largest amounts, more than that invested by nobility like the Earl of Suffolk or the Duke of Bolton; apart from few others like the Duke of Chandos, only the King and the Prince and the Princess of Wales invested more than Charteris.[36] He was one of the few who evidently profited from the South Sea venture since he was still a large investor in December 1723 and his fortune was still intact: in 1723 the newspapers tell of how 'A Gentleman of a very large Estate is soliciting daily for a Pardon for a Rape committed by him lately in Scotland' (*London Journal*, 5/1/1723). In 1730 he was in trouble over another rape – the victim being Anne Bond – and his holdings of South Sea stock became public knowledge once more. One journal tells of the seizing of his estate worth above £100,000, 'including several Mannors and estates in *Lancashire*', and five or six thousand pounds of South Sea stock (*Political State of Great-Britain, XXXIX, p. 323*). Another reports that Charteris went to South Sea House accompanied by the Sheriffs of London and High Bailiff of Westminster to pay his Composition money by selling South Sea stock to the value of £8,300 (*Fog's Weekly Journal*, 29/8/1730; 5/9/1730).

Charteris was therefore perceived by contemporaries not merely as a debauched rake but as an unscrupulous and extremely wealthy businessman who squeezed and robbed the defenceless. One story that was being circulated concerned his activities as a fraudulent landlord: he apparently directed an unsuspecting drover to rest his cattle overnight in an enclosure let to one of his indigent tenants who owed him rent; the next day Charteris seized the cattle of the innocent drover and sold them, claiming that since they were on the land rented by the tenant they were, as far as Charteris was concerned, the tenant's property and so liable to be sold to pay off the tenant's debts. It is no wonder that his dealings with whores is described in business jargon – 'goods', 'Bill of Parcel', *etcetera* – for he had become a symbol of the vicious commercial values operating in Walpole's Britain. Mother Needham, who was associated with Charteris in Hogarth's print and elsewhere, was also perceived in a commercial light: at her death her coffin, it was said, resting on eight gallon casks of Geneva wine, was lined with pawnbrokers bills, and the funeral room hung with tallymen's notes.[37]

Whilst the common whores and thieves were being hung or transported for their petty crimes, Charteris was using his wealth and position to escape punishment. He had friends in high places who screened him or interceded with the authorities on his behalf. At his trial for the rape of Anne Bond, people of quality like the Dukes of Manchester and Argyle and Sir Robert Clifton (who was later to be embarrassed over his involvement in the Charitable Corporation)[38] were in attendance. Dr Mead, the royal physician, visited him in prison and the Earl of Weems used his influence at Court to get a royal pardon for Charteris. Such a miscarriage of justice seemed to typify Walpole's reign, in which great villains could find refuge, even encouragement in Britain. The Opposition charge that Britain under Walpole had become 'the *Asylum* of *publick Plunderers ...a secure Harbour* for GREAT Villains to ride at safety in' remained to the end of his career.[39] Charteris' superiority over the processes of the law appeared to be a reflection of Walpole's own position: one of the most frequent charges against the latter concerned his alleged abuses of the law and immunity from prosecution.

Further Walpolian symbolism can be attached to Charteris in terms of the latter's employment of pimps who lingered at inns and taverns to spy out prospective country virgins arriving in London – Hogarth's picture shows one of these spies, John Gourlay. Walpole had attracted notoriety over his network of secret-service political spies positioned in Britain and Europe; these were frequently described as his 'pimps', hence phrases like 'Pimps, Spies, Informers' in anti-Walpole newspapers. In the *Beggar's Opera* Peachum and his gang of thieves and pimps are quite possibly a hint at Walpole's spy system. In any case Walpole, in the guise of various villains in many satirical plays, was either described as a super pimp himself or else as a lascivious lecher. In *Polly*, the sequel to the *Beggar's Opera*, Ducat, whose sexual needs are supplied by whoremistress Mrs Trapes, is, as Parlakian says, 'clearly Walpolian in age and habits.'[40] Several plays aimed against Walpole depict sexually incontinent villains – all analogues of Walpole – as Parlakian reveals in his study of the theme: in the *Fall of Mortimer* (1731), the Walpolian villain Mortimer attempts to seduce a virtuous maid; in David Mallett's *Eurydice* (1731), Procles, the Walpolian libertine confesses to enjoyment of rape 'because it couples sexual gratification with violent possession of the unwilling woman', a statement that could manifestly be from Charteris' own mouth; Timophanes lusts after the virgin Eunisia in Benjamin Martyn's *Timolean* (1730). Walpole also appears as a lecher in satirical poems like *Sir Robert Brass: Or, The Knight of the Blazing Star* (1731). In real life the politician was noted for his appetite and zest for female company, for feasting and bacchanalia. Like Colonel Charteris and the Jew in Plate 2 of *A Harlot's Progress*, both keepers of Moll, Walpole kept a mistress, Molly Skerrett, and this illicit relationship was frequently alluded to in anti-Walpole satire.[41] In addition Walpole was accused of being a pimp to the King: the episode in *Majesty Misled, Or, The Overthrow of Civil Ministers* (1734), in which young Spencer, in the role of pander, brings a virgin to the King, is 'an episode embodying the common Opposition charge against the Prime Minister'.[42]

It should be noted too that the story of innocent country virgins being debauched and destroyed, which had been used as a metaphor of national corruption in the South Sea period, was being applied more recently to Walpole's corrupt government of England. In *The Craftsman* of January 10th, 1730, the image of a woman sexually abused then discarded is used in a discussion of Walpole's practice of bribery at elections: '*A bribed Corporation* is like a *Woman* debauch'd, and must expect to be turn'd off and left to sift for herself, when the Corrupter hath serv'd his Turn'. Again, like a 'chaste Matron' starting at a rude overture, so must a virtuous patriot respond to the offer of bribery (*The Craftsman*, 16/3/1728). Gay's *Polly* had already spoken of the ruination of the nation in terms of the ruination of a maiden, when Mrs Trapes whose occupation as a pimp is to debauch young women, compared herself to 'those who betray and ruin provinces and Countries'. Her song continued the comparison:

In Pimps and Politicians,
The Genius is the same,
Both raise their own Conditions
On others Guilt and Shame.
....
Each a secret Commerce drives,
First corrupts and then connives,
And by his Neighbours Vices thrives.

The metaphor was also applied in a satirical poem[43] narrating the progress of an idealistic patriot who, resolving to 'pull Corruption down', gets elected to Parliament only to succumb to Walpole's inducements and to become as corrupt as the rest; his transformation and degeneration are described in terms of the seduction and prostitution of a country maiden:

So the plain Country Girl, untainted,
Nor yet with wicked Man acquainted,
Starts at the first lewd Application,
Tho' warm perhaps ьy Inclination,
And swears she would not with the King
For all the World, do *such a Thing*;
But when, with long assiduous Art,
Damon hath once seduc'd her Heart,
She learns her Lesson in a Trice,
And justifies the pleasing Vice,
Calls it a natural, harmless Passion,
Implanted from our first Creation,
Holds there's no Sin between clean Sheets,
And lies with every Man she meets.

The metaphor persists in anti-Walpole satire at least until 1743 when Fielding, echoing similar sentiments, compares the 'Debauching of a Member of the House of Commons from his Principles' to the debauching of a woman from her 'lovely State of virgin Simplicity and Innocence' (*The Life of Mr Jonathan Wild*, Bk 2, Ch. 12). In Hogarth's *A Harlot's Progress* therefore, given the prevalence of imagery, we can speculate that there are possible anti-Walpole implications in the story of the seduction and destruction of its country heroine. Charteris corrupts Moll as Walpole his country. A parallel between Walpole striving to conquer Britannia and Charteris reaching after Venus was made in two prints of 1730. The first (*B.M. Satires* No. 1842) showed Walpole trampling on the hydra of discord and ascending a monument to Britannia; the second (*B.M. Satires* No. 1841) showed Charteris stepping on moneybags on his way to sexual delights with Venus and her damsels.

Granted that in Plate I Charteris is representative, as he was to contemporaries, of all the corrupt agencies operating under Walpole, Moll can then be interpreted as a modern, flesh-and-blood version of Britannia. Hogarth's work is concerned with more than the fate of the individual; there is a wider framework of references, the harlot being used 'to reveal the villainies and hypocrisies of society', as Kunzle puts it.[44] Moll's symbolic nature is evident from the date of her death, September 2nd (inscribed on the coffin-plate in Plate 6) which is the anniversary of the Fire in London: her personal destruction is seen in the wider context of national upheaval and civil strife, Hogarth picking up again the theme of national catastrophe originally in his *South Sea Scheme* print with its symbolic Monument. His dating may have been inspired by the fact that the year of Charteris' birth was symbolically given as that of the year of the Fire of London, 1666 (*The History of Colonel Francis Ch-rtr-s*, London, c. 1730, p.7), though the Colonel was in reality born in 1675. Another influence may be the imagery of fire in descriptions of Charteris' desires – he prefers, for instance, strong vigorous sexual wenches who could *'work like a Parish Engine at a Conflagration'* (*Some Authentick Memoirs, op.cit.*, p.10) The language and imagery of fire are present throughout *A Harlot's Progress* – in Plate I, Charteris, 'fired with lust' at the sight of the fresh country virgin, is like a heated animal; Plate 2 sees Moll 'playing with fire' by keeping a secret lover, and hot liquid scalding the Jew's foot; in Plate 3 is the imagery of pouring liquids again, and a half burnt-out candle beside Moll's bed signifying her dire future; in Plate 5 she is consumed by the fevers of venereal disease, the open fire beside which she expires, the piece of raw flesh being toasted by her son, and the ash, the shovel and pieces of coal lying scattered on the floor, indicating her burnt-out physical condition; in the funeral scene, her life has been extinguished but lust survives: the liquid spilling on the priest's lap will not put out his sexual fires.

If the Fire of London reference in Plate 6 puts Moll's individual progress in the wider framework of civil upheaval and destruction, the confrontation in Plate 1 between the powerful Lancaster landlord (Charteris' extensive property in Lancashire was repeatedly revealed in 1730 in the accounts of his trial for rape)[45] and the defenceless York maiden (the wagon's inscription, 'York', tells of her Yorkshire origins) provides another more distant historical context of strife, the War of the Roses: most prominent on Moll's breast is a white rose of York. In that struggle between the nobility it was the common people who suffered extensive destruction, some hundred thousand common soldiers dying in the prolonged conflict. *A Harlot's Progress*, like much in Hogarth, is concerned with the suffering of the commoner at the hands of the 'great', and later he was to evoke another historical event of civil disturbance (the Peasants' Revolt) in conveying the theme: in Plate 8 of *Industry and Idleness*, Goodchild, the future Lord Mayor, and his mighty companions are seen feasting, whilst the poor, who come literally cap in hand, are barred from entrance to the banqueting hall; the statue of the Medieval Lord Mayor, Walworth, holding the dagger that slew the peasant Wat Tyler, reinforces the idea of the historical and continuing deprivation and repression of the common people. With regards to *A Harlot's Progress* the allusions to civil strife have possible political reference in the context of the repeated attacks on Walpole for dividing the country into warring factions for his own profit – *The Craftsman* repeatedly accused Walpole of promoting disunity, encouraging the country to divide into parties so as to weaken it. Much space was given, in that journal, to the expounding of Bolinbroke's *Dissertation on Parties*, aimed against Walpole. *The Craftsman* also constantly compared Walpole's Britain to previous eras of civil turmoil and civil war – the reigns of Edward II, Richard II, Henry VII, the Stuarts, Cromwell, *etcetera*. Classical periods (the reign of Pericles) as well as fictional events (civil war between the Noodles and the Numsculs in the Kingdom of Timbutan) were also evoked as analogues of Walpole's Britain. According to *The Craftsman*, the result of Walpole's reign is a nation divided into the powerful rich and the helpless poor – 'excessive riches in private

Coffers, and extreme Poverty amongst the Generality of the People'.[46]

Moll, then, has a status beyond that of a mere individual whore. The very title of the series tends to elevate her story into the realms of history. Bindman[47] has indicated the various 'progresses' that lie behind *A Harlot's Progress* – the *Pilgrim's Progress* and the 'moral journey of the soul towards salvation or perdition'; the geographical progress of the Lord Mayor's Procession or that of the Condemned Criminal from Newgate to Tyburn – but omits the idea of the 'Progress' as a Royal journey, as in the verse of Addison cited by Dr Johnson in his Dictionary's definition of the word:

> O may I live to hail the day
> When the glad nation shall survey
> Their sovereign through his wide command
> Passing in progress o'er the land.

Moll's 'progress' through the streets of London reveals only dirt and decay, there is none of the sense of national glamour and glory derived from pictures of Royal 'progresses' or processions. What Hogarth has done is to take official 'symbolism' and to strip it of dignity. This satiric treatment occurs elsewhere, in his *Masquerade Ticket* (1727), for instance, where the unicorn and lion, supporters of the Royal Arms, are shown lolling on their backs in an obscene manner (*Figure 39*), or more subtly in *Marriage à la Mode* Plate 5,

Figure 39: William Hogarth: *Masquerade Ticket* (detail)

where the wall-picture of a strumpet with a squirrel perched on her hand echoes the pictures of Queens holding up squirrels in playing card iconography (*Figures 40-41*).[48]

Figure 40: William Hogarth: *Marriage à la Mode* (detail)

Figure 41: Anon: *Playing Card*

Triumphs from feilds of Blood ye Sythian Lady brought.
But ore' mankind their Eys have mightier Conquest wrought.

Moll's journey in her lowly wagon alludes possibly to the Progress of Royalty in the Coach of State and to the related imagery of Britannia in her coach, which Hogarth was to parody in Plate 3 of the *Election Series* – there the coach has broken down, the horses rearing up in an undignified manner whilst the coachman keeps the rein with his foot instead of his hands; Britannia tugs at the communication cord but her drivers (that is, the politicians) are too busy playing cards to bother. (*Figure 42*) Britannia is a recurring figure in Hogarth's works, from the *Lottery* (c.1721) where she is a more or less conventional figure, to Plate 8 of *A Rake's Progress* (retouched in 1763) where she is a dishevelled and lunatic woman. Another version of her occurs in Plate 2 of the *Election Series* (*Figure 43*) in the female seated on the British lion: the Cornucopia associated with Britannia

Figure 42: William Hogarth: *An Election [The Polling]*

Figure 43: William Hogarth: *An Election*
[*Canvassing for Votes*]

has become here a horde of coins with which she has been bribed; Hogarth has made her into an inn-hostess, and in view of the keys dangling from her waist (also the keys of State) and the ladies of leisure on the balcony, a whoremistress no doubt. The whore being fondled, in the funeral scene of *A Harlot's Progress*, may also be viewed as a vulgarizing of the figure of Britannia, her sprig of rosemary echoing the olive branch Britannia normally holds up, and the plate at her feet Britannia's shield.[49] The reading of Hogarth's Moll as Britannia accords with Britannia's depiction in eighteenth century political prints as a youthful, simple maiden who is persecuted or violated:

> Satirists and propagandists tried to convey in Britannia the idea of virtuous innocence. Again and again the prints show her as an innocent, abused, insulted, cozened.[50]

In one print of 1721 relating to South Sea (*B.M. Satires*, No. 1710) she is sprawled out naked on the ground, dying: in others, she appears as a naked whore being whipped or being raped by men, being defecated upon, and so on. Similar sexual imagery is to be found in political literature around the time of *A Harlot's Progress:* in one anti-Walpole satirical essay entitled *The Dream,* Britannia, once a beautiful white-robed maiden presiding in a lush, rural environment degenerates under Walpole's government into a rope dancer like those common women performing in fairgrounds. She becomes the 'Sport of all Nations', prurient men crowding to watch her and struggling to topple her into their arms. When finally rescued by a band of patriots she is weak and dishevelled, 'her Strength wasted, her Treasure lost, and her Garments rent'.[51] Thomson in a 1729 poem aimed against Walpole's peace policy, has Britannia, violated by Spain, in a state of mourning:

> Bare was her throbbing bosom to the gale,
> That, hoarse and hollow, from the bleak surge blew;
> Loose flowed her tresses; rent her azure robe.
> Hung o'er the deep from her majestic brow
> She tore the laurel, and she tore the bay.
> Nor ceased the copious grief to bathe her cheek;
> Nor ceased her sobs to murmur to the main.
> (*Britannia*, l. 4-10)

(b) Plate 2: Thomas Woolston, Bishop Gibson and Sir Robert Walpole – Hogarth's satire on the political Church (Figure 34)

On the wall of Moll's apartment hangs two portraits, one of which is of Thomas Woolston, a famed deistical writer of the times. According to Nichols a proof plate of Plate 2 of *A Harlot's Progress* had the words 'Mr Woolston' inscribed under one portrait but this with other details had, for unspecified reasons, been removed before the finished prints were delivered to subscribers.[52] The identification of Woolston remained however in the copy, authorized by Hogarth, printed for Giles King as well as in the version printed for John Bowles at the Black Horse in Cornhill. Grub Street pamphlets based on Hogarth's series also maintained the identification. Hogarth's citing of Woolston may be merely a means of attracting popularity by mention of someone who was very much in the news at the time; this was one of the tricks of his trade. In the 1730s, Woolston's name was being capitalized by everyone and mentioned in the most irrelevant contexts, and Hogarth's reference may have been part of this parasitic process.[53] There is slightly more logic though in Hogarth's case, in so far as contemporaries had linked Woolston to Colonel Charteris, the previous villain of Plate 1. One writer in 1730 claimed that Woolston had been invited to dine with Charteris at his house in Hanover Square and to bring with him his famous book, *Discourses on the*

Miracles. Charteris and Woolston then became warm companions: 'The *Divine* and the *Debauchee* it seems were excellent good Company, having discharged no less than seven Flasks between them'. The Colonel afterward 'gave his Word and Honour' that he would patronise Woolston, make him his chaplain and provide him with any gift that fell into his hands.[54] These allegations were grossly untrue and poor Woolston who was in all sorts of trouble with the authorities at the time had to insert an advertisement in a national newspaper to repudiate them:

> Whereas the Author of a Pamphlet, call'd authentick Memoirs of the Life of Col. Ch...s, Rape Master General of Great Britain, has inserted a Story of the Conversation the Col. is supposed to have had with me. These are therefore to certify the Publick, that the said Story is entirely False and Groundless.
> Witness my Hand, Thomas Woolston[55]

Woolston, a generous, honest soul was pressed by sympathisers, some of whom denied the allegations on his behalf, to take legal action, but in his compassion for the libellous Grub Street hack (who after all had to make a living somehow), he refused to do so and was lauded for this charitable attitude.[56] It was perhaps out of fear of any such prosecution that Hogarth, deciding to avoid mentioning Charteris and Woolston in one context, erased Woolston from his picture.

Another incidental reason for the initial inclusion of Woolston in Plate 2 is because in his theological writing he had adopted the persona of a Jew to present his deistical arguments: according to Woolston a Jewish rabbi had written letters to him on the subject of the Resurrection pointing out the supposed absurdities and flaws in the Christian story, and he Woolston was merely voicing the scepticism of the Rabbi. Of course people saw through Woolston's persona, but in any case a furious pamphlet battle ensued against Woolston's rabbi.[57] In *A Harlot's Progress* it is understandable that the Jew (Moll's keeper) should have bought Woolston's portrait – from Dadridge or Vanderbank, both of whom had painted him – Woolston appearing to sympathise with Jewish arguments against Christianity.

A more intriguing explanation though for Hogarth's allusion to Woolston is that he forms an important reference point in the overall satire against the Church – and by extension, against Walpole – present in *A Harlot's Progress*. Contemporaries were fully aware of the fierce personal battle being waged between Bishop Gibson (the Bishop of London), and Woolston – in one of the paintings on the wall of Plate 2 the Christian Bishop stabbing the Jewish Uzzah for desecrating the Ark of the Covenant refers not only to Christian Moll's betrayal of her Jewish keeper (who is being 'stabbed', through a trick of perspective, by the escaping lover's stick) but perhaps also to the tremendous violence with which Gibson attacked Woolston for the latter's supposed desecration of the Gospel miracles. The deeper reason for Gibson's spleen was not theological but much more practical: the instinctive self-defensive reaction of a creature under attack. According to Woolston, who was prosecuted by blasphemy, beaten up in prison, and who spent his last years confined to the Rules of the King's Bench prison, Gibson had called upon the civil powers to repress him because he had attacked the Bishop's avarice and had called 'for the Abolition of an hired and establish'd Priesthood', the removal of the financial privileges of the 'monopolists' of religion.[58] Woolston's allegorization of the Gospel stories was more than an academic theological exercise, but deeply satirical: for instance the story of Christ driving the buyers and sellers out of the temple is interpreted as a prophecy of the future ejection of greedy Bishops, Priests and Deacons from Christ's Church. He interprets the story of the woman miraculously cured of an issue of blood in an anticlerical way: the woman is the Church and the physicians upon whom she has vainly spent all her money are

> the *Clergy*, our Practitioners in Theological Physick [who, for nearly 2,000 years] have received of the Church vast Fees, Stipends, and Gratuities (for before that Time her *Doctors* prescrib'd freely) to take care of her Health and Welfare; but unless God provide in due time a Medicine of his own, she is likely to continue in a diseased and sorrowful Condition for all of them.[59]

Such attacks on the 'Quack-Doctors of the *Clergy*'[60] were political and led to Gibson's attack on Woolston for being, in the latter's own words, 'false to the Author of our Faith, and to the present Government'. They correspond with similar sentiments being voiced in Opposition journals about the corrupt Church and its support of Walpole. *Fog's Weekly Journal* for instance attacks the clergy as hireling slaves who suck up to Ministers of State for financial gain, using such descriptions as the 'Prelate grasping after Pluralities, [who] spend[s] his Time in cringing to the Great, in Hopes of a good Translation'. (10/4/1731)

Walpole's opportunity to exert influence over the Church through personal appointments came in 1723 when five Bishops all died in the space of seven months , and a sixth, Lord Atterbury, Bishop of Rochester, was found guilty of high treason and exiled. From then on Walpole had the Church firmly in his control, working closely with Gibson to cement the relationship. Gibson became the ecclesiastic adviser of the Whig ministry, 'the primary aim of all his activities [being] to reconcile the Church to the Whig Administration', as his biographer put it.[61] It was for this reason that Gibson earned the contemporary title of 'Walpole's Pope'; their relationship was described less politely in terms of a criminal brotherhood between 'Receiver and Thief'.[62] Together they worked out a scheme for the control of the two universities by means of gifts, placements and rewards, thereby further consolidating clerical servility to the Government. Gibson later helped to save Walpole's skin when the

Opposition, scenting blood after the tremendous defeat of Walpole's Excise scheme earlier in the year, disinterred the issue of the South Sea frauds with the hope of finally trapping and destroying the wily politician. Gibson heeded the cry for help and rallied the Lord Bishops to frustrate the House of Lords proposed enquiry into the way the expropriated estates of the ex-South Sea directors had been disposed of. Such loyalty to the Government was to be vigorously satirized:

> Consider the Church is your Rock of Defence,
> Your S[outh] Sea Escape in your Memory cherish,
> When sinking you cry'd, help L[or]ds, or I perish.[63]

By 1731/2 Gibson was so fully identified with the Government that any attack on him inevitably constituted an attack on Walpole. Hence Hogarth's satirical reference to him in *A Harlot's Progress* undoubtedly has political implications. In Plate 3 Moll's use of Gibson's pastoral letters (which were written in reaction to Woolston's essays) as a paper to wrap up butter expresses Hogarth's contempt for Gibson.[64] In Plate I the clergyman ignores Mother Needham's seduction of Moll, his back turned against them. He is too eager reading a letter to Bishop Gibson, from whom he hopes to gain a place, to notice the leading astray of one of his flock.[65] His situation and the horse that he rides summon up the political phrase 'jockeying for position' and perhaps point to Gibson and the satirical equestrian imagery applied in descriptions of his ambition to become the Archbishop of Canterbury. Hogarth's depiction of the inattention of the Clergy to their moral duties (the priest in Plate 6 is also careless of Moll) is a recognisable criticism of the Church at a time when it was seen to be more involved in wordly than in spiritual affairs. In the 1730s the Church was active in a heated public battle to preserve its revenues from tithes, vigorously opposing a 1731 Parliamentary Bill aimed at preventing suits for tithes in certain situations. The energy and dedication with which the Church launched itself in the effort to preserve its economic privileges led to extensive satire on the clergy. It is hard to decide, one writer declares, whether they 'shewed more Acuteness in Defence of the *Christian Religion*, or the *great Case of Tythes*'. There is an obvious reference to the Walpole-Gibson alliance in the description of priests 'so busy in Shoals at Westminster-Hall, so constant at *Levees*, so assiduous in *Drawing-Rooms*, and so ambitious for Power...'.[66] The bitter feelings of 1720 against a Church shamefully involved in South Sea matters were once again unleashed in the 1730s over its political and materialist positions, and Hogarth, topical as ever, incorporated them in his pictures.

If Charteris in *A Harlot's Progress* represents one of the secular forces ranged against the common people, then Gibson who stood for the established Church, is a symbol of clerical tyranny. The tithes debate had expressed the fear of civil strife and division, some seeing the matter in terms of the few rich versus the mass of the common poor: as in Catholic Europe a Church victory in the tithes issue would mean that property would be 'wholly *engrossed* by a *few contemptible Miscreants*, and the *greatest* Part of the People *eaten out of their Estates*, nay excluded from ever retrieving them, by a *Succession* of *Ecclesiastical Catterpillars*, who impiously call themselves, *Successors to the Apostles*'.[67] The spectre of Papacy, with its associations in England of civil turmoil, of the great fire of 1666, of the sense of a nation divided between priestly rich and secular poor, and so on, is broadly reflected in Hogarth's series which also refers to civil strife and to the Fire of London, and sees things in terms of the 'great' versus the poor. The anti-Catholic element in *A Harlot's Progress* lies in its extensive parody of Catholic iconography: in Plate I, Moll is the Virgin Mary, Mother Needham, Elizabeth, and Charteris, Zachariah, the figures arranged as in Old Masters paintings of the *Meeting of Mary and Elizabeth*; in Plate 6 Hogarth quotes *The Last Supper*, his picture amounting also to a gross parody of a Lamentation group. (Hogarth's contempt for English connoisseurs who spent lavish sums on Old Masters – 'the shiploads of dead Christs and Madonnas' arriving from France and Italy – was bound up with his anti-Papist attitudes). In 1720 and the years immediately following, anti-Catholic feeling in England (and in Hogarth's pictures of the period) was a product of hostility to the Catholic convert John Law and his French Mississippi scheme which disastrously influenced the South Sea company; in the 1730s such a feeling had a new political application, against Walpole and his control, through Gibson, of the Church. Walpole's 'soft' approach to France and Spain and supposed friendship with French and Spanish ministers led to innuendoes about his secret Catholic sympathies. These were reinforced by what was deemed his tyrannical political rule over Britian, and the gush of anti-Papal emotion in the period of the Excise Bill reveals the extent to which Walpole was imaged as a Catholic-type despot (*B.M. Satires* Nos. 1928, 1937 *etc.*) Finally the charge of Papacy originated from Walpole's practice of bribery which reduced the nation to fawning and slavery, the sort that, according to the traditional English view, operated in Catholic countries. He is described as a 'Lord Peter in the State' in an essay in *The Craftsman* (21/9/1728) dealing with the situation that arises 'When temporal Ministers become Lay-Popes'. The cry of 'slavery' was constantly raised in Opposition literature:[68] Walpole had, it was claimed, reduced Britain to a state of abject servility by his keeping of a standing army, by the tough application of the libel laws, by his system of promotion and rewards and so on. A passage from Henry Brooke's *Gustavus Vasa* (1739) sum up the sentiments expressed from the late 1720s onwards regarding Walpole's administration of the country:

He has debauch'd the Genius of our Country,

And rides triumphant, while her Captive Sons
Await his Nod, the silken Slaves of Pleasure,
Or fetter'd in their Fears.

Inevitably the 'slavery' of Britons under Walpole was compared to
African slavery, to the fate of Guinea blacks at the hands of greedy
British traders.[69] *A Harlot's Progress* contains many images of 'slavery'
– in Plate 1 there are extensive indications of bondage. Moll, on
arrival in town is hemmed in by the buildings and by people
determined to exploit her. The language of the African slave trade
had already been evoked in describing Charteris and his pimps, the
latter being like 'Factors' employed by a slave dealer, 'Procurators and
Purveyors for *Flesh*'.[70] The idea of confinement is conveyed too by the
objects in Hogarth's print – the box tied up with rope, the padlocked,
coffin-like trunk with its prominent series of nails, the sturdy
encircling hoops of the barrel and the string that has strangled the
goose's neck, the last reflecting on Mother Needham's gesture to
Moll's neck and chin which are also tied, by her necklace and by the
lappets of her hat. Other details in Plate I like the women wedged in
the York wagon or the string of buttons running down the coat of
Charteris' pimp, John Gourlay, which resembles a chain originating
from his wrist, reinforce the sense of 'enslavement'. Gourlay's hands
are crossed in a gesture evocative of 'slavery' and correspond to the
position of Moll's hands: (*Figures 44-45*): both are 'slaves' of sexual

Figure 44: William
Hogarth: *A Harlot's
Progress Plate 1* (detail)

Figure 45: William
Hogarth: *A Harlot's
Progress Plate 1* (detail)

and economic powers and designs, one to Charteris, the other to Mother Needham. Moll's tiny scissors dangling from her bag is a poignant detail in its ineffectiveness against the 'enslaving' process initiated against her. In Plate 2 the presence of the black houseboy carries on the idea of 'slavery' – Moll has now become a 'slave' to luxury with the Jew as her new keeper, but like the horse in the previous Plate she is straining at the leash, kicking over the tea-table as the horse has disturbed the buckets. Plates 3 and 4 see her arrest and committal to Bridewell, the black prisoner in the latter scene again conveying the idea of 'slavery'. In the following Plates Moll is totally swallowed up, trapped, confined to the point where, in the coffin, she has ceased to be visible. Details of blocked doorways, rooms deprived of sunlight with crisscrossed windows like prison bars, hands wedged in stocks, leg irons, lice caught and squashed between fingernails and hemp for rope-making all add up to the overwhelming feeling of 'enslavement', which has possible anti-Walpolian resonance in the context of the Opposition's widespread appication of the 'slavery' metaphor to describe Walpole's Britain.

As to Bishop Gibson it is reasonable to conclude that Hogarth's reference to him are meant to hint at his role in the system of 'slavery' represented in *A Harlot's Progress*. In attacking Woolston Gibson had evoked the 'Popery and Slavery' slogan[71] but it was Gibson rather than Woolston who was seen by contemporaries in terms of tyranny, as the designation 'Walpole's Pope' indicates. The author of *A History of the Priesthood, Ancient and Modern* (1737) tells how the critics 'paint him as a man insufferably proud, arrogant, haughty, ravenous and no less vindictive than the Grand Inqusitor of God...' (p.60). In 1729, 'John Wickliffe' writing against religious persecution, such as that of Woolston, by the Walpolian clergy, sees Gibson and his type as representative of cruel authority over the common people – his book is ironically dedicated to such religious despots but also hints at the secular ones who were making news at the time, men like Colonel Charteris and Sir John Gonson, the magistrate of Plate 3 of *A Harlot's Progress*:

> To All such as love to plague and harass the rest of Mankind, by what Names or Titles soever dignified or distinguished: whether they be most Reverend Fathers in God...Lord Bishop, or other inferior Priests or Deacons; Grand-Jurymen, Petit-Jurymen, or other inferior Ministers of Justice: Colonels, Lieutenant-Colonels, or other inferior Dealers in Blood and Slaughter...[72]

A few years later, Richard Savage's poem, the title of which, *The Progress Of A Divine*, alluded to Hogarth's series, attacked Gibson – and by implication, Walpole – as enslaver and exploiter of the poor:

> His *Servants*...Hard has Fate their Lot decreed:
> They toil like Horses, like Camelions feed.
> *Sunday*, no Sabbath, is in *Labour* spent,

And *Christmas* renders 'em as lean as Lent.
Him, long, nor faithful Services engage;
See 'em *dismiss'd* in Sickness, or in *Age!* (1.255f)

It can be said then that *A Harlot's Progress* perception of a brutally commercial society in which the 'great' feed off then discard the common people, owes its inspiration to the system of ideas (or 'public patterns of thought' as Paulson puts it) prevailing in the literature and prints aimed against Walpole and his administration, from the late 1720s onwards.

Before leaving Plate 2 and the political meaning generated by the references to Woolston and Gibson, the figure of the Jewish merchant needs to be analysed. Jews were a traditional target of Christian hostility and their situation had not altered much in eighteenth century Britain in so far as they were still liable to be bashed about by the mob at the slightest excuse. Hogarth is shamelessly and greedily capitalizing on popular prejudice against the Jew by depicting him in a contemptuous light: he is the type of image that would boost sales among the populace, both among its hooligan as well as its respectable classes. The situation of the Jew and his Christian mistress in Plate 2 of *A Harlot's Progress* is an immediately recognisable one to the spectator accustomed to reading saucy literature about English courtesans bubbling their Jewish keepers. There was a popular belief that Jews were licentious creatures much addicted to patronage of Christian whores whom they attracted by their ready commercial wealth, although there was an anti-semite law expressedly prohibiting such contact.[73] 'Madam was once kept by a Jew; and baiting their religion, to women they are a good sort of people', Mrs Slammekin confesses, in *The Beggar's Opera* (Act II, Scene 4). Reports from the newspapers of 1723 indicate the supposed extent of Jewish involvement with Christian women:

> The Vienna Letters mention, that a Jew at Presburg, who had been lately concerned with a Christian Woman, was fined a Thousand Florins, and obliged to ride through the City upon a Hog. If every one of that Tribe here, that has taken the same Liberty, was to be punished in like manner, 'tis believed the Streets of this populous City would be filled with Jews so mounted.[74]

Hogarth's Jew, however, is perhaps more than a sexual symbol, his significance extending into the world of contemporary politics. Walpole, in spite of the support received from the established Church, had no personal religious animosity towards dissenters, and he was sometimes criticized for his seeming overtolerance of religious differences. His attitude to Jews was also one of tolerance and formed yet another focal point for Opposition satire – the issue of Jewish naturalization. This issue dated from the previous century, economists like Sir Josiah Child proposing naturalization on the practical grounds that Jews had a beneficial contribution to make to the financial well-being of Britain, whilst others argued that such aliens would, by their competition, prove harmful to British traders. In the years preceding the South Sea Bubble the question of naturalization was once again discussed, John Toland arguing for it out of humane as well as economic considerations ('Have we not all one Father...'; 'the encrease of people encreases import and export ...'), his attitude provoking hostile response and the presentation of opposite views.[75] What may have attracted Hogarth's attention to the naturalization question was the criticism voiced over Jewish membership of Masonic Lodges. The Constitution of the Freemansons allowed for Jewish participation but in the early 1730s people were discussing the propriety of granting such facilities to non-British and non-Protestants, their sentiments and the related opinions about naturalization being recorded in the public journals.[76] Walpole around this time was being linked with Jews: one poem dated about 1728 accuses him of betraying his country's religion by being agreeable to the naturalization of Jews, implying that, like Judas, he was bought out by them:

A glorious Knight has now design'd
Your Race from Curse to free
Nor is there sure in all your kind
A verier *Jew* than he.

....

The Gospel, like its Lord, is sold
Nor gives the Price Offence,
Make it but a Ship-load of Gold
Instead of Silver pence.[77]

Another poem, 'A New Song. To an old Tune', dating around the same period, refers again to Walpole's friendship with Jews:

For your fav'ring the *Quaker*, and settling the *Jew*,
The Merit whereof, give the Devil his Due,
Is yours, aye, and that without Irony too.[78].

As late as 1754, in the furore caused by the Jew Naturalization Bill, Walpole, long dead, was being vilified for his symaphy for the Jewish cause: one satirical print has Walpole greeting Henry Pelham in Hell and praising the latter's attempt to naturalize Jews as his supreme wickedness (*B.M. Satires* No. 3264). Hogarth's Jew is noticeably 'naturalized' in his association with a Christian woman, in the manner of his taking tea (he holds the cup as fashionably as any young aristocrat), his distinctly non-Jewish clean-shaven chin, and his elegant wig: Hogarth deliberately puts the Jew's hat under his arm to draw attention to the wig. (The ill-fitting wig – a few strands of hair are still visible – reveals that the Jew is not yet wholly 'naturalized'.) As to his clothing, again, it reveals his acclimatization: he has, as Quennell put it, 'assumed the embroidered coat, ruffled shirt and crisply curled wig of a metropolitan man of the world'.[79]. Observations of traditional Jews on London's streets or acquaintance with literature on Jews would have informed Hogarth as to their traditional customs and habits, enabling him to include details in his representation of the Jew that would signify departure from these customs and habits. In the latter case one work published in 1728 helps to pinpoint such areas of departure: it tells for example that Jews 'take great Care not to fling any Bread or Meat on the Ground, lest they should be thought to despise the Gift of God'.[80]. The scattering of food (tea) in Hogarth's picture may be an ironic visualization of such a passage – the Jew's hand grasps the rich tea-table and appears to follow the tumbling silver tea-pot but more out of consideration of their material value than out of any religious ideal, such an interpretation of Hogarth's picture allowable in view of the traditional concept of the greed of the Jew, as well as by the rake-like spread of his fingers, signifying avarice. The book makes much mention of the special clothes worn by Jews (no wool or linen, in obedience to *Leviticus* XIX) and their particular way of dressing, all of which Hogarth's Jew is at odds with. Jews also have a 'particular way of dressing their meats' and Moll's sartorial elegance, in contrast to her appearance in Plate 1, may be an ironic reflection of this information. Hogarth's Jew therefore is in most respects a very non-traditional figure, his 'naturalization' perhaps pointing to the conconsequences of Walpole's policy towards Jews.

Like Gibson who was described as 'a *Son* of *Levi* right' because of his avarice and ambition, Walpole was insulted by such satirical epithets as 'Rabbi Robin' for his sharp practices, and 'Prime Minister to King Solomon'.[81] George II, Walpole's master and co-conspirator in iniquity according to the Opposition, was frequently called 'Solomon', perhaps because of his action, which made history and created a considerable stir at the time, of attending a Jewish wedding when he was the Prince of Wales. In 1727 rich Jewish merchants lent his wife Caroline a great amount of costly jewellery for her coronation attire.[82] Walpole's administration also had the support of City Jews, including Sampson Gideon who, Paulson suggests in a footnote, may be the very Jew represented in Hogarth's picture. Gideon was an extremely wealthy businessman, a stockjobbing magnate who in his lifetime rose to become one of the directors of the Bank of England, having, like Bishop Gibson, owned large quantities of Bank stock. He was later to be known as a financial adviser to Henry Pelham and was satirized in the 1753 anti-naturalization prints and possibly in Hogarth's *Election* Series, but he was also connected to the early ministry of Sir Robert Walpole. His relationship with Walpole possibly dates from the 1720s when it was said that he helped the politician in the financial arrangements undertaken to salvage public credit after the bursting of the South Sea Bubble. Walpole in turn aided him through a special Act of Parliament legalizing his purchase of a portion of land.[83] If the figure in Plate 2 is Gideon then his closeness to Walpole's administration would reinforce the political elements in Hogarth's satire on the Jew.

(c) Plate 3: Sir John Gonson and Sir Robert Walpole; the theme of the 'Great' versus the common people (Figure 35)

Hogarth's picture tells of Moll's imminent arrest by a magistrate, identified by contemporaries as Sir John Gonson, who, around this time, had become a household name through his tireless suppression of brothels and gambling dens. Hogarth depicts him in a satirical light – as Bindman observes, as Gonson enters the room he appears to waver momentarily 'as if caught by lust at the sight of the harlot's seductive presence, for it was an old saw that such moralizing zeal was essentially prurient'. Gonson's gesture of secrecy also links him to the escaping lover in Plate 2: both use Moll sexually, one physically, the other vicariously. The plagiarists and Grub Street hacks who produced their own versions of *A Harlot's Progress* did not miss the point about Gonson's sexual interest: 'She's a very pretty girl, I had much ado to maintain my magisterial gravity in committing her,' Justice Mittimus confesses in one such publication. Another describes how:

> Sir *John*, and all his *Myrmidons* appear'd,
> With Clubs, and Staves equipt, a num'rous Herd.
> The surly Knight, intrepid, led the Van,
> But stopping short, her curious Form to scan,
> The Beauties of her Air, her Face, and Shape,
> Did on his Zeal well nigh commit a Rape;
> Soften'd his Rage, and almost drew him in,
> To fall a Victim to the pleasing Sin;
> Till re-assembling all his scatter'd Powers,
> 'Courage, my Boys!' he cry'd, 'the Fort is ours...'[84]

The true classical reference however is not to Myrmidons surprising the unconscious town of Troy but to satyrs surprising the sleeping or unconscious nymph (Moll is accordingly in bed). There is an ironic allusion too to the iconography of the Adoration of the Shepherds, the point being that Gonson's adoration of Moll is of a sexual nature. Hogarth in all this is hinting that Judge and victim are equally sinful, but that the former is shielded from prosecution through his social position while he damns the latter, the poorer, more defenceless sort, for the same crime. The anti-Walpole theme of the 'great' versus the 'small' is being continued here.

In picking on Gonson rather than on any of the other London magistrates, Hogarth may be exploiting not only the greater fame of the man but also the fact that he was seen by contemporaries as one of Walpole's creatures. Gonson was knighted at the beginning of

Walpole's reign, on May 14th, 1721,[85] and his support of Walpole's administration become obvious to all through his charges to the Grand Juries of Westminster which was thunderous and widely reported events. He has 'opened the Sessions with his usual Eloquence, by giving a most learned and elaborate Charge to the Grand Jury,' one journal recorded (*Political State of Great Britain*, XLV, 1731, p.84) using more respectful language than Pope who in *Satires of Donne Versified*, IX, described the magistrate's addresses as 'the Storm of Gonson's lungs'. In Hogarth's picture Gonson's gesture of silence is ironic, indicative of his normal heated garrulity; it also adds a tremendous aural tension to the picture, for Moll is unaware of the impending verbal clatter about her ears. Gonson's charges were supererogatory in zeal and content – this being manifest by comparison to the addresses of other Justices –[86] and they amounted to a strenuously subservient defence of Walpole's government. He used the Bench to disseminate Government propaganda, as Gibson used the Pulpit for similar purposes:

> It is apparent to any one, that will but reflect upon all these Particulars, That in no Age hath there ever been in this Nation, or in any other, a more universally Glorious Administration, that we now enjoy under his Sacred Majesty King GEORGE the Second... As to the Treasure and publick Credit of the Nation, Was it ever rais'd to such a Height before, as it is now? Or the Purse ever in better Hands? Such a Confidence the People have in the public Management, and are so well satisfied, that what we pay is punctually apply'd to the Service to which it is appropriated, and the whole manag'd with such exquisite Conduct and Frugality, by those honourable Persons who preside over the Treasury, that never were taxes more freely complied with, nor such large Sums raised so speedily, and at so low an Interest...'[87]

Such a passage could easily have come from the mischievous pen of a Nathaniel Mist or a Nicholas Amhurst (anti-Government writers) but it is a sample typical of Gonson's speeches, delivered without irony or innuendo. It is no wonder that there was widespread cynicism about the law and frequent attacks upon Walpole for his buying out of Judges and Jurymen who had degenerated into businessmen and tools to Ministers. *The Craftsman* (5/8/1732) in a bitter essay on corrupt and overpowerful Justices tell how they have become political slaves interested only in the acquisition of money, to the detriment of the common people: 'Oaths and Warrants are sold, like Sugar and Plumbs, to all Comers, and the poor People are encouraged to harass one another, on purpose to increase his Worship's Income'.

Hogarth would have been particularly conscious of Gonson's politics in so far as they related to his own craft and business, for sizeable passages in the magistrate's charges were given over to the need to suppress and punish satire against Walpole's administration:

> there is one Thing more, which I must at this Time particularly recommend to you, and that is, to present the Authors, Printers, and Publishers of all Libels. It is a

shame to our Nation, that there should be any Persons belonging to it so little sensible of the Happiness which we enjoy, as to libel and disturb such a King, and such an Administration; yet this Offence is now grown so common, that if a Man goes into a Coffee-House, it is uncertain whether he lays his Hands upon a News-Paper, or a Libel.

(*Five Charges, op. cit.,* pp.35-6)

Gonson did not stop at verbal satire but urged prosecution of pictorial satire too, 'Dumb Scandal' or 'Scandal by Pictures or by Signs' as he puts it (*ibid.,* p.37). Hogarth would have undoubtedly perceived this as a direct threat to his potential livelihood as a pictorial satirist. The full political import of Gonson's speeches has to be understood in the content of widespread discussion at the time about the freedom of the press, a heated issue which brought charges from the Opposition that Walpole was stifling dissent either by buying out journals and employing hack editors, or else by harassing hostile writers with lawsuits. Gonson's position in the freedom of the press debate is obvious from the above quotation from his speech, and his denunciation of one issue of Nathaniel Mist's newspaper – 'the Malignity of the Villanous One of Mist's Journal of the 24th of August last' – which had been prosecuted for its supposedly libellous content. (Bishop Gibson had already declared himself against Nathaniel Mist, a leading Opposition journalist, in urging that 'some method be taken to convince Mist and his brethren that they are not allowed ... to make their Tory friends merry at our expense').[88] As Goldgar states (though without supporting evidence), Gonson's charges 'voiced the official dismay at the ubiquity of opposition propaganda'.[89] The satirical journals in turn attack Justices as instruments of tyranny in their tightening up of the interpretation as to what constituted libel. They evoke the good old days before Walpole when invective could flow more freely, unimpeded by fear of lawsuit, when

> to call a Man Murderer, was construed a Murderer of Horses; and of later Days, to say a Man had the *Pox* was held not actionable, unless he further explain'd himself, as by saying he got it from a yellow hair'd Wench, in *Moorfields;* and of late days, to say of a Justice of Peace, that he was a *Dunce, a Blockhead, and a Beetle-headed Justice,* was not held actionable.

The last reference here, in *Fog's Weekly Journal* of April 11th, 1730 is almost certainly to Gonson who had only a few days before delivered one of his 'extraordinary Charge[s], as usual, to the *Grand Jury,* against *Libellers,* seditious *Pamphleteers,* &c.' (*Craftsman,* 4/4/1730), which was reported as usual, in the newspapers. On reflection there is possibly an additional meaning to the detail in *A Harlot's Progress* Plate 3, of Gonson with his hand at his mouth: Hogarth may easily be hinting at Gonson's suppression of political speech, a meaning beneath the obvious signification of Gonson's gesture of silence.
Apart from his charges to the Westminster Juries, another passion-

ate and publicly debated issue around the time of the conception of Hogarth's series which linked Gonson to Walpole was that regarding Dunkirk. In the early part of 1730 rumours spread in England that the strategic French Port was being rebuilt and refortified in spite of Article 9 of the Treaty of Utrecht (1713) which ordered its demolition. The Opposition immediately launched attacks on Walpole for not having the nation's interest at heart and for his peace policy towards France. The French monarch in response to an overture from Walpole dispatched a French officer, Captain Blandinière, to Dunkirk to survey the situation and to reassure the British, but Walpole's critics accused him of bribing Blandinière so that the latter would overlook any new fortifications at Dunkirk and produce a report favourable to Walpole. Gonson became involved in the affair when in March 1730 affidavits were sworn before him by two mariners, George Collcott and Robert Jones, in which they claimed that they had been eye-witnesses to a conspiracy against Walpole, led by Lord Bolinbroke; the conspiracy was said to have been aimed against Walpole's peace policy and involved the spreading of false news in Britain about the repairing and re-opening of Dunkirk. The Opposition dismissed the affidavits as a ministerial ploy to protect Walpole from popular outrage and to bolster his political standing. Gonson was criticised for hearing the affidavits, the implication being that he was in Walpole's pay, part of Walpole's system of deceit:

> But who engaged them to go and make their Affidavits before that learned and eloquent Magistrate and Chairman, Sir J– G–, and who has been at the Expense of printing, publishing and dispersing them from the post-office, this Affidavit so *ministerially* penn'd, I confess, is more than I can guess. I conceive, it cannot be the worthy Magistrate before-named, who at this own Charge so frequently refreshes the Publick with his eloquent Orations, in some of which a particular Charge is given against the heinous Sin of Perjury, for, I am sorry to say it, the chief point aim'd to be proved by this Affidavit, happens to be unluckily false...[90]

The polite adjectives describing Gonson are of course ironic for Nathaniel Mist (the editor of the newspaper bearing this article) and Gonson were sworn enemies. Later in the same article Gonson comes in for more attack, the writer declaring that he

> cannot forbear making a wish, that the worshipful Sir J---G---wou'd have been so good as to have taken the Affidavit of some Person who had been Eye Witness of what Monsieur Blandinier has done, and that the like Methods were used to acquaint the Publick.

Gonson therefore is not merely a harlot-hunting Justice but a symbol of Walpolian tyranny, his political sympathies being manifest to contemporaries from his charges and his involvement in the Dunkirk cover-up. In this he is the equivalent of Charteris, Gibson and the Jew. In Hogarth's picture there are obvious links between all these characters in terms of their exploitative and destructive relationship with Moll/Britannia. They were also connected in various ways in actual life. Bishop Gibson had called upon the civil powers to repress writers like Woolston who criticized the Church on theological and political grounds, when declaring that 'the Duty of the Civil Magistrate, at all Times, [is] to take care that Religion be not treated in a *ludicrous* or *reproachful* Manner, and effectually to discourage such Books and Writings.' Gonson showed obedience to the Bishop when charging his Grand Juries to try to 'find out these detestable Authors [of 'all Books and Pamphlets wrote against Religion, or the Sacred Scriptures'], Present the Printers and Pubiishers'.[91] His political sympathy for Gibson can be gathered from his excessive praise of the Bishops when speaking of

> the great Learning, Piety, truly Christian Moderation, extensive Zeal, and Christian Charity of those most Reverend Prelates, who now adorn the Mitre, [who] will, in all human probability, raise the Lustre and Reputation of the Church of *England* to such a Degree, that as the Steddiness of his Majesty's Counsels, and the Wisdom of his Administration justly entitles our Nation at present to hold the first Rank, so shall our Church...become a Praise in the whole Earth.
> (*Five Charges, op.cit.*, pp.47,48)

As to the Jew, Gonson was linked to him in a satirical ballad of the time (around 1731/2) dealing with the investigation of South Sea directors by a Committee of Fifteen:

> Six *Bishops*, Seven *Doctors*, One *Justice*, One, *Jew*,
> All qualify'd, *righteous*, upright Men and true;
> Are humbly propos'd to be the *Inspectors*
> Of the doubtful Affairs of the *South-Sea Directors:*
> For *Bishops*, who doubts but they are all *good!*
> And *Doctors*, for certain, are of as true *Blood.*
> For *G--son's* great *Justice* you need not to doubt,
> A Thousand Poor Devils would gladly come out
> From *Newgate* and *Bridewell* to prove it all true
> For *G--son's* as *honest* almost as a *Jew:*
> And *Jewish Uprightness* there's none can gainsay,
> They ne'er take a *Bribe*, nor ever *Betray:*
> These things being prov'd, 'tis hope'd you will chuse 'em,
> For *the Devil is in you*, if you can refuse 'em.[92]

The connection between Gonson and Charteris is one that minds critical of the processes of the law would have made, for whilst Charteris was raping at will and being pardoned for his crimes, magistrates like Gonson were in hot pursuit of common whores who were less able, through poverty and lack of political influence, to defend themselves: news of Gonson's arrests were interspersed among reports of Charteris' triumph over justice, in the journals. According to one account of the career of Charteris, a magistrate once shielded him from prosecution for rape. He seduced a country girl in

London but her father made an application to the Justice of Peace for a warrant to arrest him. 'The Colonel being a Man of Fortune, the Magistrate sent him Information of the Charge, before he issued out his Warrant'. Charteris bribed the magistrate to bully the girl's father, a simple man, into withdrawing his suit: the magistrate

> advising the poor Man to make himself as Easy as possible, alleging that the Colonel being a Great Man, would over-power him, if he should Commence a suit against him, and therefore he had better sit down contented with the first loss Etc.[93]

The fact that Charteris, as the newspapers tell, was on the Commission of the Peace for the County Palatine of Lancaster, and that his father-in-law was a Senator of the College of Justice would have reinforced cynicism about the ideals of Justice that Gonson (who once described the law as a process of ensuring that the 'Weak' did not become 'a Prey to the Strong') was supposed to represent.[94] In Hogarth's series the spatial positioning of Charteris in Plate I and Gonson in Plate 3 are similar enough to point to a connection between them, as Paulson notes when writing of the 'parallel, between Gonson and his assistants emerging from their doorway and Charteris and his pimp emerging from theirs'.[95] They are both lingering about doorways, lusting at the sight of Moll, one about to entice her inside the building, the other to drag her outside.

It is therefore possible to conclude that there is a perceptible logic, in the context of contemporary politics, in Gonson's inclusion in *A Harlot's Progress*. His role as prosecutor of Moll carries on the anti-Walpole theme, set up in Plate I by the presence of Charteris, of the 'great' versus the 'small', a theme that had a basis in real events. Early in 1731 a crowd gathered outside Walpole's house in Arlington Street and hurled abuse at his steward Jenkins; three men were subsequently committed to Bridewell to hard labour for inciting the people.[96] His most famous confrontation with the populace came in 1733 in the jubilation that followed the defeat of his Excise Bill. There was rejoicing in the streets, burning of bonfires and effigies, and ringing of bells:

> Nor was he only attack'd in Effigie, but even insulted in his Person, as he went thro' the Court of Requests... for rude Hands were laid upon him, and had he not been defended by some of his Friends, the Consequences might have been something too shocking to think of.[97]

Charteris too was a target of popular anger – a mob besieged and stoned his house on hearing rumours that he had kidnapped a young woman and was holding her captive there; 'a whole posse of Constables, Headboroughs, Etc. came to keep the peace' on that occasion. At his death 'the people of his neighbourhood attacked the hearse, strewed it with refuse, tried to tear his body from the coffin, and threw the carcasses of dogs and cats into the tomb'.[98] With regard to Bishop Gibson, his involvement in the Society for the Reformation of Manners, a body that brought thousands of prosecutions against the common people for petty crimes like swearing, and none against great villains like Charteris for raping, would hardly have contributed to his popularity. As for Gonson he became a symbol of tyranny through his harassment of the defenceless and down-and-outs. In one poem that appeared in *The Craftsman*, dealing with oppression of the people by Walpole, by lawyers, doctors and directors of the Charitable Corporation, Gonson is cited in an unfavourable context. The poem attacks Walpole for keeping a standing army, which is a drain on the country's resources as well as an instrument of tyranny; it is not as if the standing army is an aid to Gonson's operation against whores and gamblers for he is capable of executing the job himself:

> Nor does Sir *John* require your Aid,
> But wishes you would mind your Trade,
> Whilst he alone can serve you;
> For by his own unwearied pains
> *Sharpers* and *Whores* He leads in Chains,
> And triumphs o'er *Moll* Harvey.
> (*Craftsman*, 22/7/1732)

Here Gonson's activities are seen as part of the picture of general tyranny operating in Walpole's Britain. Like Walpole and Charteris he became 'the Butt of the Malice and Revenge of all the Vagrants in Town', with threats to his life and the stoning or beating of his officers and constables as they attempted to execute their warrants. On one occasion Gonson himself was cornered in Fetter Lane by two malcontent gamesters and he had to be rescued. His response to such resentment was to strengthen the power of his policemen by enabling them to beat up people at the expense of the state: he applied to Lord Harrington, Secretary of State, for the King to grant permission for the Treasury to undertake the costs of lawsuits brought against his men by the populace. On August 11th, 1730, his request was granted, Lord Harrington writing to inform Gonson that his Majesty, agreeing with the determination to stamp down on vice

> has been graciously pleased to direct me to issue out Orders to his Solicitor of the Treasury, to defend at his Majesty's Expence, any Suits that shall be so commenced against any Constable, Headborough etc.[99]

(The King, so zealous in the cause of purity and morality, meanwhile pardoned Charteris.) Gonson had earlier urged strict prosecution of libellers of magistrates, as a means of stifling dissent (*Five Charges, op cit.*, p. 106).

All these facts were publicly known, carried in the newspapers of the day, and even the most mundane mind would have realized that Gonson was directing his energies against the wrong people, his lower-class victims being less guilty than their social superiors. The point was made by contemporaries when reporting on Gonson's prosecutions: the common people are basically virtuous, they become corrupt only through the bad example of 'the Rich and the Powerful'. The dissolute and irreligious lifestyles of Gentlemen are a bad influence, for 'the little Rogues put in Practice what they have learned at the Tables of the Great'. The clergy are to blame for the neglect of their duty of educating the poor, their overriding concern instead being to ensure a good dinner from their parishioners. Finally, the increase of roguery is put down to the increase of lawyers who encourage crime so that they can profit from it; they find loopholes in the law whereby villains escape to commit more crimes and more fees for lawyers:

> I am of the Opinion that it fares with Law as with Religion: when there are too many Priests in a Country, they neglect the Principle end of their Institution, which is to inculcate the Principles of true Religion, and Morality into the Vulgar and Ignorant, and in place thereof, they fall a splitting, dividing, expounding, and confounding Articles of Faith and Principles of Religion, in such a Manner that the People are either all set by the Ears together, or become so perplext with hard Words and Mysteries, that no Principle of Real Religion or Virtue is left among them.[100]

There is a broad affinity with such attitudes in Plate 3 of *A Harlot's Progress*. Moll's use of Gibson's pastoral letters as a butter dish indicate the irrelevance to the poor of the theological controversy between the established Church and the Deists; it is butter that the people find more important than broadsheet bickering.

The juxtaposition of the portraits of Dr Sacheverell and Gay's Captain Macheath on the wall of Moll's dwelling, in Plate 3, amounts to an equation between the Statesman – Bishop and the common thief, such an equation also having political resonance in view of the literary structure, established by *The Beggar's Opera*, of comparing Walpole and his men to a gang of common robbers.[101]

> Two Heads beneath the shatter'd Windows hung,
> *Sacheverel's*, and *Mackheath's*, remain unsung,
> Both Doctor's in their Way, both high renown'd,
> Their Merits like, and with like Honours crown'd;
> Vast plund'rers both, and excellently pair'd,
> Who not for Country, nor for Conscience car'd,
> This, a Lay-Brother, fam'd for Whores and Wine,
> And that, a Robber of the Race divine;
> This, for our Coin, set up a bold Pretence,
> That, for our Laws, and Liberties, and Sense.
> (B.M. *Satires* No.2064)

Such a passage immediately recalls the frequent descriptions of

Walpole as a tyrant using the law to subvert the law, and the word 'Plunderers' would have instantly brought to mind the politician, being a favourite term in Opposition satire. Like the journalist cited above, Hogarth is saying that it is the 'great' who provide sordid precedents for the poor (Moll in Plates 2 and 3 is clearly imitating the vices and habits of aristocratic Ladies) though it is the latter who invariably end up in jail. By depicting Moll's whoring and thieving he is really pointing to the immorality of her social superiors, of Walpole and Walpolian villains. Gonson is one such villain and tyrant, and in depicting him satirically Hogarth is reassuming previous attitudes to Justices, from such prints as *Royalty, Episcopacy and Law* (1724) in which the law in its crushing power is seen as a tool of political and business interests, and from such paintings as that of Isaac Shard (around 1731), 'a prodigious penurious Kt...a Magistrate of the City of London' sentencing to death a hungry dog that 'had stolne from his Honours kitching a pitieous lean scraggy shoulder of Mouton'[102] (the dog here, as elsewhere in Hogarth, being a symbol of the lower class, the have-nots and social outcasts.)

(d) Plate 4: The Prison Warder and Sir Robert Wapole; the theme of the 'Great' versus the common people continued (Figure 36)

The prison scene of *A Harlot's Progress*, with its brutal warder and general squalor illustrates a social issue that was a matter of considerable public discussion in this period – the conditions and administration of the nation's prisons. It was an issue that was of particular significance to Hogarth in view of the prison experiences of his impoverished father. In 1726 an essay was published highly critical of prison warders, drawing attention to the 'Miseries and Torments poor Prisoners, for Debt, have suffered, as *Starving, Dungeons, Chains, Whippings, Beatings,* breaking their *Limbs...*'[103] A few years later, outrage at the death of the architect Robert Castell in the Fleet prison led to Parliamentary investigation into the prison system, which revealed shocking evidence of the despotism of Officers, the appalling distress of prisoners and the abuse of the charitable funds that existed to relieve them. Many tracts were issued detailing the tragic experiences of the people unfortunate enough to have landed in jail. The names of two prison officials in particular emerged from all this public inquiry, those of John Huggins and Thomas Bambridge who subsequently both stood trial for various misdemeanours. The trial of Charteris for the rape of Anne Bond was attracting public attention at about the same time, as was Gonson's prosecution of whores, and his part in the Dunkirk affair. In November and December 1730 the newspapers report on the court case brought against John Huggins over the death of Edward Arne who had perished in prison after brutal treatment by the warder.

Huggins, represented by no less than six lawyers, was found not guilty by Lord Chief Justice Raymond on a technicality, 'it appearing that Mr Huggins acted by Deputy; and that tho' in Civil Cases the Principal is answerable for his Deputy, yet in Criminal Affairs he was not; whereupon Mr Huggins was discharged.' A week later came news of Charteris' repossession of all his estates previously forfeited by his conviction for rape, due to the King's pardon, 'so that we may say he is now as good a Man as he was before.' One journal pointedly juxtaposes news of Mr Huggins' acquittal in the Court of the King's bench with that of the sentencing by the same Court of a common prostitute, Moll Freeman, to hard labour in Bridewell. It was also Justice Raymond who had earlier in the year acquitted Bambridge for the murder of the inmate Robert Castell, whilst the highwayman James Dalton (his hatbox lies on top of Moll's bed, in *A Harlot's Progress* Plate 3) a week earlier had been sentenced to three years' imprisonment for attempting to rob Dr Mead, the Royal Physician. Soon after this event another petty thief Francis Hackabout was arrested and committed to Newgate; he was then sentenced to death at the Old Bailey with other malefactors (they all received sentences on the same occasion) including Charteris (who was of course subsequently pardoned). Justice Raymond in the same year punished leading opponents of Walpole, finding Francklin, the printer of *The Craftsman*, guilty of libel and sentencing Woolston to prison (plus a fine of £100, a considerable sum in those days); Woolston at his trial declared that he was being prosecuted not for any 'blasphemy' in his writings, but because he had dwelt at length on *'hireling Priests...here, my Lord,...the Shoe pinches.'*[104]

Inevitably, the seeming unfairness of the various legal judgements whereby the great and wealthy escaped punishment whilst the poorer sort or the politically dangerous people were fined, imprisoned, transported or hanged, was put down to corruption under Walpole's rule. One popular ballad, *On Colonel Francisco Rape-master General of Great Britain* links Charteris, Bambridge and Huggins in terms of Walpole's screening of the three of them from the effects of justice:

> The same that for *Huggins* was once in a Fright,
> For whom *Acton* and *Bambridge* will swear by this Light,
> To a Rogue in Distress he is stil'd a *True Knight*,
> Which no body can deny.

Bambridge's assertion of his own self-created authority, his disregard or abuse of the Law, as if he were superior to it, recalled Walpole's own attitudes and activities. Even though reprimanded by Judges, Bambridge nevertheless loaded his prisoners with irons; he brushed aside *Habeas Corput* writs (Walpole courted notoriety in 1723 by suspending for a while *Habeas Corpus*, an act which the Opposition press constantly reminded the public of), punished prisoners on no authority but his own and used the law at times to secure his position. *The Craftsman* of May 10th, 1729 carries a satirical account of Bambridge in which his character and actions are seen to be analogous to Walpole's. Bambridge is described as 'this Great Minister', a phrase calculated to evoke Walpole's name; a year earlier *The Craftsman* (17/2/1728) had represented *The Beggar's Opera's* Lockit (the prison warder) as 'the Keeper or Prime Minister of Newgate'. Bambridge's creation of an armed force, kept in his own pay, within the Fleet prison, is compared to Walpole's standing army, both being used to terrorise the people and to extort money from them. *The Craftsman* points to Walpole's justification of his standing army when it presents Bambridge's explanation as to why he kept a private force in the Fleet Prison:

> for all these military Preparations, he gives the best political Reasons imaginable: First, by pleading his Prerogative, that it is done by his own Authority; and secondly, by declaring the Ends and necessity of these wise Provisions, and their Usefulness to the Publick; that it is done for preserving the Quiet and Safety of his People.

The tyranny, arbitrary power and maladministration of the prison warder are made to reflect upon the condition of Britain ruled by Walpole, the exposure of which 'is by no means to be called *Libelling the State,* but, on the contrary, ought to be look'd on, as the genuine Issue of a public Spirit', *The Craftsman* declares with obvious reference to Walpole's practice of snuffing out criticism by applying the laws of libel. Other points of similarity between the two men lie in Bambridge's 'great Name and Titles' – 'Guardiaaus, sive Custos Prisonae de la Flete; Solicitor of Solicitors; Councellor of Councellors, Founder of Dundgeons and noble Manufacturer of Iron Bolts and Manacles.' Here, Walpole's many titles and decorations are being parodied, a common opposition point of attack (hence the satiric sobriquets given to Walpole like 'Sir Blue String' and 'Sir Blue Ribbon'). The prison warder's manipulation of prisoners and employment of servants is related to the politican's management of gifts and sinecures:

> Mr B. seems to be well experienc'd, and improv'd in the Management and Disposition of Public Accounts and Revenues...I like his Skill and Conduct in the Disposal and Ingrossing of the several Places of Trust and Profit, within his Jurisdiction. All these were Venal, that they might be exactly like his own. He assum'd the Power of changing Sides and Rooms, and turn'd many out of Places which they had paid for, on Purpose to be paid for them again. He took large Premiums; but gave his Dealers a Power, to reimburse themselves out of the Pockets of his Vassal.

Finally the sordid commercialism of the prison – the bleeding of fees from inmates, the illegal release of selected prisoners to commit crimes outside, portions of the profit of which had to be handed over to Bambridge, and so on – is seen as exemplifying the grotesque materialistic values presiding in a society ruled over by Walpole. Just as the metaphor of slavery, and the parallel between Englishmen in bondage and Guinea blacks, had been extensively applied by Opposition satirists in describing Walpole's reign, so Bambridge is conceived of as a slavedealer: debtors are sold into slavery to the prison warder and his deputies who 'make the most of them; to the great Encouragement of Trade and Commerce' (the last phrase strongly evocative of the typical kind of justification of the African slave trade made by its practitioners).

In view of the connections made by contemporary satirists between Walpole and villains like Charteris, Bambridge and Huggins in terms of the facility granted to such tyrants to commit crimes against the people with impunity, it is reasonable to conclude that Hogarth's prison scene, depicting the suffering of the common sort, including one African prisoner, at the hands of a merciless warder (an analogue of Bambridge or Huggins), whilst the greater villains, Charteris, Needham and the Jew, are absent, invites political interpretation.

Hogarth's picture reveals the inhumane commercialism of the prison system. Moll is about to be stripped of the fine clothes given to her by her former Jewish keeper, most of which will end up in the possession of her new keeper, the prison warder. The process of exploitation begun by Charteris in Plate 1 continues here. So far Charteris and the Jew had used her sexually, Mother Needham economically. Gonson had derived surreptitious sexual pleasure in persecuting her, as well as cash profit, for like Mother Needham his trade and income centred around prostitutes. Hogarth in a previous painting, *A Woman Swearing A [Bastard] Child* had represented the idea of a Justice making money from the sexual looseness of women, as the caption to Joseph Sympson's engraving of the painting told:

Here Justice triumphs in his Elbow Chair
And makes his Market of the trading Fair.

Through knowledge of Sympson's print which was publicly advertised in *The Craftsman* in 1730 (14/2), observers of *A Harlot's Progress* would have understood the economic angle to Gonson's activities and the ironic connection between him and Mother Needham through their common capitalization of Moll's body. It was to Gonson's acquisition of wealth from prostitution that *The Craftsman* (4/9/1731) hinted cynically in one essay: defending Pulteney (a leading figure of the Opposition) against charges of profiting from public office, the essayist describes how Pulteney is now an ordinary citizen, reduced to the station of a private country gentleman, 'and alas! Sir John Gonson is now a greater Man than He.' Gonson's financial position can be gathered from Ship Insurance and South Sea subscription lists that include his name; his profit from prostitution was not only monetary but in the form of election to public offices – as a Commissioner appointed by Parliament for building a bridge across the Thames from Putney to Fulham, as a Colonel of Tower Hamlets, and so on.[105] Gonson reappears in Hogarth's prison scene, the inmates expressing their hatred of him by drawing his effigy hanging from a gallows, on the door in background. His hands are drawn as rakes, recalling the rake-like spread of the Jew's fingers in Plate 2 as he grasps after the falling silverware: both men are identified in their avarice. Like Gonson the prison warder also benefits sexually and economically from Moll. His threat to beat her recalls Moll's flagellation of her clients (her birch is displayed in the previous scene); the flogging of whores in prison had an element of sexual sadism in it, a common contemporary observation.[106] There is a financial stimulus too in the use of the rod on Moll for the hemp she beats will be sold to merchants for the making of rope and sailcloth, the money accruing to the prison warder. Additional income would be obtained from the transportation to the colonies of some of the female inmates, a process that was big business:

> In the transportation of felons, a whole hierarchy, from courtly secretaries and grave judges down to the jailors and turnkeys, insisted on having a share of the spoils ... The merchants and justices were in the habit of straining the law to increase the number of felons who could be transported to the sugar plantations they owned in the West Indies. They would terrify petty offenders with the prospect of hanging and then induce them to plead for transportation.[107]

The prominent presence of the black woman in *A Harlot's Progress* prison scene further reminds the observer of the financial exploitation of whores through transportation and colonization. Like *The Beggar's Opera* which extends beyond London to the colonies, (hence references to colonies within the play as well as the setting of its sequel *Polly* in the West Indian settlements), Hogarth's representation of the economic environment of London extends, by implication, to the overseas British Empire – such an extension inevitable and logical since British economic life was inextricably bound up with colonial trade. On reflection the pipe Gonson (in the effigy on the prison door) smokes, whilst making him a symbol of death (smoking in seventeenth and eighteenth century literature, and in some of Hogarth's prints, being a metaphor for the process of dying), may also have economic import, for tobacco was a major colonial product, reaping vast revenues for British merchants. Tobacco was also one of the chief means, used instead of money, by which American and West Indian planters purchased female convicts who were sold to them as mistresses. The lonely and wifeless planters, sexually gratified by these transported prostitutes were thereby encouraged to stay on and to continue the economic development of the colonies, which in turn provided wealth to Britian; the children issuing from these sexual alliances were also economically beneficial, through the increase of the population of the colonies, population, as the maxim ran, being the wealth of a country.[108] Gonson, in his pipe smoking, may therefore be seen as a figure very relevant to the commercial system indicated in the prison scene. The rope and sailcloth manufactured from the hemp beaten by the harlots also indicate colonial commerce since they were essential naval stores – hence the many agricultural manuals at the time on the cultivation of hemp and the schemes for raising hemp in the colonies.

As to the slogans about 'industry' in Plate 4 ('Better to Work than Stand thus' and 'The Wages of Idleness' inscribed on the whipping post and stocks) they add to the environment of ugly commercialism depicted throughout Hogarth's series, and they may have an anti-Walpole slant. In Gay's *Polly* which like its predecessor *The Beggar's Opera* deals with the worlds of the 'great' and the 'small' and the different codes of behaviour applying to those worlds, 'industry' is seen as being expected only from the poor: 'Honest industry! I have heard talk of it indeed among the common people, but all great genius's are above it' (*Polly*, Act 3, Sc.3). Gay's presentation of the Walpolian system in which the great and rich plunder and recline in luxury whilst the poor are expected to work hard, to be physically and morally upright ('Morals and Honesty leave to the Poor') accords with the depiction of social injustices and imbalances in *A Harlot's Progress*. The 'industry' slogans may also be topical references to the Charitable Corporation whose collapse, perceived by contemporaries as exemplifying the fraud thriving under Walpole's reign, coincided with the publication of Hogarth's series. The Corporation existed theoretically for the benefit of the 'industrious poor' (its full title was 'The Charitable Corporation for the Relief of the Industrious Poor') though in reality it financed a different type of 'industry', the greedy, energetic speculations and stockjobbery of its proprietors who were scornfully described afterwards as 'Gentlemen of the Industry' and as 'these virtuous and industrious Gentlemen' (*The Craftsman*, 29/1/1732; 20/5/1732). 'Industry' was the sacred ideal in an age of commerce and much literature – essays, poems, plays – was devoted towards encouraging the menial classes to work and produce. Hogarth is being cynical in quoting stock sentiments about the virtue of labour, showing its merciless and one-sided application to the poor. The prison warder is, like the Charitable Corporation director, a gentleman of industry, plundering the poor on the excuse that by encouraging them to work he is thus fulfilling a socially beneficial ('charitable') duty. Indeed Moll, the York girl, beating hemp in jail may be a cynical comment on a well-publicized 'charitable' scheme of 1730 'laid before the Lords of the Treasury, for erecting several Workhouses for improving the making of Sail Cloth [from Hemp] in the County of York, for the better regulating and employing the poor in the said County.' The journal quoted here (*Fog's Weekly Journal*, 14/

3/1730) had two paragraphs before mentioned the rumours of Charteris being pardoned for rape (through the kindness of the Court) and the juxtaposition of such news items would in itself have made a mind like Hogarth's become cynical about 'charity'. Finally Hogarth may have in mind too the fact that Gonson was being lauded for his contribution to industry. In April 1731 a petition by a great number of tradesmen was delivered to the Court thanking Gonson and the other Justices for their good work in clearing the streets of unproductive and socially useless 'vermin' – vagabonds, beggars, cripples and the rest.[109] In the previous year Gonson has been thanked for his campaign against whores (whose main sin was not moral but economic – the seduction of apprentices and consequent disruption of trade, as in Lillo's *London Merchant*) – among those that ought to be grateful to Gonson are 'Shopkeepers and others who have any Children, Apprentices or Servants within the Bills of Mortality'.[110]

(e) Plates 5 and 6: The Quack and Sir Robert Walpole
(Figures 37-38)

The sexual-economic exploitation of Moll continues, this time at the hands of doctors who take money from her on the pretence of being able to cure her of venereal disease, and the undertaker who, with the parson, not only makes money (funeral fees) from Moll's death but use the occasion for sexual frolic with the attendant whores. The heartless commercialism of the funeral scene is depicted comically in the action of one of the female mourners who covers her left eye with a handkerchief in a gesture of grief but whose right eye eagerly watches the valuable mourning ring being put on her finger; another whore picks the undertaker's pocket whilst allowing him to seduce her.

The quack was a traditional symbol of deceit – 'the eighteenth-century embodiment of riches got by humbug and chicane'[111] – but around the time of *A Harlot's Progress* he had become in political satire *exclusively* evocative of Walpole. Walpole as a quack was a satiric literary structure established at the inception of *The Craftsman* in 1726 – the journal repeatedly told of, or mockingly advertised, the cures of 'Dr Robin Sublimate' for the body politic; the image persisted in dozens of plays, ballads, popular prints and Opposition newspapers.[112] Walpole was represented as a quack deceiving simple country people by his false pills and medicines (his 'grand Specificks') which he claimed was effectual in curing poverty, the pox, and so forth. His 'Mercury' however kills the patient, not heals; his 'Specifick is a meer Imposition of the People'.[113] Hogarth's picture, because of the ubiquity of the quack symbolism in anti-Walpole satire, opens itself to political interpretation. Its depiction of the enrichment of the doctors through the destruction of Moll (the mercury given to her kills instead of healing her) recalls the widespread accusation made against Walpole, that he raised himself and accummulated wealth by the despoilation of the country and its people: he 'preys upon human Gore, and fattens Himself upon the Vitals of his Country.' (*The Craftsman*, 4/5/1728) A print dating around 1735 (*B.M. Satires* No. 2268) politicizes Hogarth's picture of quackery (*Figure 46*). It shows the physicians of state administering their medicine of gold to an expiring patient, with Walpole supervising the operation. Prints on the wall include two of Hogarth's engravings – *Midnight Modern Conversation* and *A Harlot's Progress* Plate 3.

Figure 46: Anon: *The Physicians of State*

A Harlot's Progress then, through the presence of Charteris, Gibson, the Jew, Gonson, the prison warder and the quacks, consistently invites political innuendo, these characters all being associated with Walpole in varied ways. Apart from the human elements, even objects in Hogarth's series, in retrospect, may have anti-Walpole connotation – for instance the forage being devoured by the lean, hungry horse in Plate 1. The horse is already heavily laden with meaning – its hunger tells of the parsimony of its priestly owner, and of the lustful salivation of Charteris at the sight of Moll; it also anticipates Moll's later situation in Plate 5, her salivation (of a different sort from Charteris') under the direction of the quacks, and her starved body – Moll has by this time become toothless, her dentures lying discarded on a piece of paper. Her progress, of feeding upon or being fed to others in terms of sex and money, is nearly over. The condition of the horse initiates the chain of ideas regarding feeding or parasitic processes – images of eating and drinking, or pouring liquids, pork being roasted, butter, a dead goose outside a tavern, *etcetera*, abound in *A Harlot's Progress*. The detail though, in Plate I, of the starved horse ridden by a political clergyman may convey meaning outside the immediate narrative context, amounting to a swipe at Walpole. In 1712, Walpole, previously Secretary of War in Queen Anne's reign, had been imprisoned, amidst considerable public stir, for the mismanagement of a Scottish forage contract and alleged embezzlement of funds relating to the contract.[124] It was Walpole's job to ensure the supply of forage to army horses quartered in Scotland and the contract was given to the Lord Provost of Edinburgh, after consultation between Walpole and Scottish officials, Scottish army officers like Colonel Douglas having a financial share in the undertaking. Walpole was accused of authorizing a deal disadvantageous to the Government, with the contractors making excessive profits, some of which ended up in Walpole's pocket. He was charged with high breach of trust and notorious corruption, and imprisoned in the Tower for a while. In Plate I of Hogarth's series the presence of the Scottish villain, Colonel Charteris, in conjunction with the detail of the starved horse and hay, would have triggered off the memory of the Forage contract to perceptive spectators. Charteris too had made money out of Scottish military affairs, in his enrollment of debtors and bankrupts for a fee into his company and pocketing of Government money from false wage claims. Both Charteris and Walpole were in trouble at about the same time over their shady dealings regarding the army in Scotland: Charteris was being investigated in the winter of 1710-11, and in February 1711, brought to Parliament where he was reprimanded by the Speaker; Walpole a few months afterwards was facing inquiry into his conduct in the Forage affair. In Plate I there is in addition much evocation and play on the word 'forage', in the actual hay, in the horse raiding (or 'foraging') it; in Charteris' hands 'foraging' through his pocket for the money to pay for Moll; in Mother Needham and John Gourlay who 'forage' for virgins at the various inns in London, or in the case of the clergyman, for a pension or place at Court. At the time of Hogarth's picture such a term had specific anti-Walpole connotation, for satirists kept reminding the public of the politician's earlier career by raking up the sordid details of the Forage scandal.[115] Certain words became odious to Walpole because of their political charge and signification, words like 'Hay' and 'Forage'. One satirist in 1731 says that he knows a person who

> changes Colour at the words Hay and Forage. A little after he conceiv'd an Aversion to the word Screen, insomuch that his Wife chang'd the Name of that useful Utensil into a Frame; but the Maid happening to call it, A rotten dirty Screen, good for nothing but to be burnt, He ask'd her what she had to do with State Affairs, and abuse great Men? and order'd her to be turn'd away. No Cure can be found for his Folly; his Phrenzy daily increases; and all the following words set him a raving; Corruption, Bribery, Pensions, Fleets, Treatises, Seville, Vienna, and fifty more.

Phrases like 'making hay whilst the sun shines' had similar satirical connotations which applied to Walpole's activities.

(f) References to Walpole elsewhere in Hogarth's work

The overwhelming impression left by *A Harlot's Progress* is of a society devoid of spiritual values and of moral direction. Moll's treatment at the hands of the soldier, priest, merchant, magistrate, warder and doctor amount to an indictment of the professional classes, the leaders of society, for the neglect of their moral duty. Hogarth is here restating the same sense of the betrayal of stewardship that his *South Sea* print of 1721 had created. In the late 1720s and throughout the 1730s there was renewed anxiety about the lack of professional standards, the betrayal of trust, the misuse of power and about corruption in high places, such a mood – and Hogarth's series reflect it – emerging from the contemplation of Walpole's activities as Prime Minister. Major and minor writers, Tories, disenchanted Whigs, or those of no party affiliation, joined in the attack on Walpole.

The general consensus of critical opinion however is that Hogarth, apart from the later period of his attack on John Wilkes and his defence of the Earl of Bute's ministry, was an a-political animal, suspicious of 'party' and of statesmen ('Great Men') in general. Wilkes himself held this view, regretting that Hogarth with *The Times* prints had entered into

> the poor politics of the faction of the day, and descending to low personal abuse, instead of instructing the world, as he could once do, by manly moral satire. Whence can proceed so surprising a change?
> (*The North Briton*, 25/9/1762)

More recently, scholars like Ronald Paulson and Derek Jarrett have stressed the political neutrality of Hogarth up to the mid-1750s.[116] Such a perception however needs considerable qualification. It is true that at first glance prints like *A Harlot's Progress* appear to be moralistic rather than political, but a deeper understanding of the period and its characters (in this case Colonel Charteris, Bishop Gibson, Sir John Gonson and others) reveals the extensive political aspects of *A Harlot's Progress* series. What Hogarth does is to give an appearance of generality to his satire by working its current political references into an older moralistic and picaresque framework (the literary traditions exemplified by *The Pilgrim's Progress*, by popular ballads on the wickedness of prostitutes, *etcetera*). The reasons for Hogarth's subtle method in the 1730s are twofold: firstly, he could not, financially, afford to shut the gates of patronage by outspoken and explicit criticism of Walpole and his affluent associates, for there were very few people in the Opposition of equivalent status as potential patrons; secondly, political satire in the 1730s was necessarily oblique and generalized. As Walpole began increasingly to bring legal prosecutions for libel against his attackers (and it must be remembered that many magistrates were his creatures), so satire became increasingly oblique and disguised, working by suggestion and innuendo. Many issues of *The Craftsman*, the leading opposition paper, were devoted to discussing the strategy of satire, whether it ought to be generalized or particularized, such discussion revealing the opposition's anxieties over prosecution.[117] 'It is necessary', *The Craftsman* declared in 1732,

> for all Authors, who have render'd Themselves obnoxious to Men in Power, and write in Fear of the Lash of the Law, to be exceedingly careful in the Choice of their Subjects, lest the Warmth of a luxuriant Imagination should hurry them into some Ideas, or Expressions, which may happen to give Offence.
> (6/5/1732)

Nicholas Amhurst, the leading journalist for *The Craftsman* explained the indirect approach that was necessary for the sake of safety:

> as long as I confine myself to General Expressions, or wrap up my Invectives against Vice in Dreams, Fables, Parallels, and Allegories, I must insist on it that I keep within the proper Bounds of a Satirist.
> (9/3/1728)

If, as Paulson states, Hogarth does not deal *openly* with political matters after 1728 as he had done in earlier works like *The South Sea Scheme* and *Royalty, Episcopacy, and Law*, then this is not due to any dramatic shift in Hogarth's attitude to politics, as Paulson implies, but rather to the increasing need to be subtle, the satirist having to rely heavily on the interpretative abilities of his 'readership'. In Hogarth's case his financial needs and responsibilities (compounded in 1729 by his entering into marriage), in conjunction with his profound fear of imprisonment (as evidenced by his obsessive depiction of prison situations), a fear no doubt originating from childhood (his father's imprisonment in the Fleet prison), would have automatically acted to temper his satire in *A Harlot's Progress*.

Another reason for the seeming lack of political references in Hogarth's work after 1728 (Paulson's date) is that by that time he abandoned engraving as his primary medium of expression. The print was the most natural vehicle for pictorial political commentary – it was relatively cheap to produce, it sold for a few pence, thus having a potentially large market, and it could be produced at a moment's notice since it paid scant attention to formal and other aesthetic niceties. Hogarth was greatly ambitious, he wanted to have the status of a serious and immortal painter and not an ephemeral hack engraver. To be a great artist he would have to delineate *character*, as opposed to dealing with *caricature*. For a painting to endure through time, and so ensure the immortal fame so desired by an ambitious young artist like Hogarth, it had to deal with universal themes; it could not limit itself exclusively to particular moments of politics. It is therefore not that Hogarth after 1728 abandoned his interests in politics but rather that he abandoned the print as his mode of expression; his concern for politics is subordinate to a wider concern for the condition of man, for he is now using paint, not ink.

After the publication of *A Harlot's Progress* the Opposition to Walpole quickly recognised the potential value of the artist to their cause. *The Craftsman*, the main Opposition paper, began to allude to his work and to mention him in a complimentary manner, as 'the ingenious Mr Hogarth';[118] Hogarth subsequently relished the application of the epithet 'ingenious' to his name. A hitherto overlooked and unrecorded fact is that in 1733, the year of the notorious Excise Scheme which nearly toppled Walpole and which saw a spate of prints and poems hostile to the Government, Hogarth's name was being connected to one popular anti-Walpole ballad, *The Projector's Looking-Glass, Being the Last Dying Words and Confession of Sir Robert Marral*. *The Craftsman* and other newspapers carried advertisements for the ballad in which it was stated that Hogarth illustrated it:

> In a few days will be published the Projector's Looking-Glass; or, the last dying Words and Confessions of Sir Robert Marrall, premier Exciseman of Great Britain, who was burnt in Fleet-Street, on Wednesday the 11th Instant; taken faithfully from his own Mouth at the Place of Execution. To which will be prefix'd his Effigies, drawn upon the Spot and curiously engraven by Mr. H-g--th.[119]

No such illustration has come to light, and it is therefore doubtful that Hogarth was at all involved; but at least the fact that hack writers were confident enough to evoke his name publicly, reveals their confidence that he would be sympathetic to their cause.

The Opposition had reasonable grounds for expecting support

from Hogarth. He had after all chosen to advertise his *Harlot's Progress* engravings in the *Craftsman* (29/1/1731-2) an act of potential significance. Only recently, in 1728/9 he had produced a picture, *Henry The Eighth And Anne Boleyn* which had inevitable political overtones in view of the innumerable comparisons made by the Opposition between the corrupt character of Cardinal Wolsey and Sir Robert Walpole. At the time of Hogarth's picture reference to Wolsey was normally a means of pointing to Walpole. In addition Hogarth had only recently illustrated scenes from the two major pieces of anti-Walpole literature of the 1720s, Swift's *Gulliver's Travels* and Gay's *The Beggar's Opera*, as well as designing the frontispiece to Fielding's *Tragedy of Tragedies* (1730/1), a play which contained satire directed against Walpole's administration.[120] Hogarth also did work for Opposition writers in the years preceding the *A Harlot's Progress*. In 1726 he illustrated Nicholas Amhurst's *Terrae-Filius* – Amhurst was the first editor of *The Craftsman*; in 1727/8 he did the frontispiece to Thomas Cooke's translation of Hesoid – Cooke was Amhurst's successor at *The Craftsman*; in 1730 he did the frontispiece to James Miller's *The Humours of Oxford* – Miller was linked with the Opposition and wrote anti-Walpole pamphlets.[121]

Hogarth's work after *A Harlot's Progress* continues to refer to Walpole in a variety of ways. In his next satirical series, *A Rake's Progress,* for instance (*Figures 23-30*), Rakewell's character and habits are so analogous to Walpole's that a re-examination of the meaning of the series is called for. Like Walpole, Rakewell is associated with Oxford. In Plate I Hogarth indicates that Rakewell is an Oxford student by the inscription on one of the love-letters from Rakewell to Sarah Young, held in the apron of Sarah's irate mother – 'To Mrs Sarah Young in Oxford'. A major series of anti-Walpole prints published around 1733 entitled *R-b-n's Progress In Eight Scenes; From His first Coming up from Oxford to London to his present Situation (B.M. Satires* No. 1938) started with Walpole being blessed by Fortune, just as Plate 1 of *A Rake's Progress* showed Rakewell's inheritance of a fortune. Rakewell's rise to aristocratic status from humble middle-class beginnings (Plate 2) has potential political import when one recalls that throughout the 1730s Walpole was being derided as a social upstart, his lowly origin frequently alluded to mockingly in satirical literature.[122] Like Walpole, who became notoriously 'cultured', Rakewell announces his entry into the state of aristocracy by collecting Old Masters and by supporting the Opera (Plate 2).[113] Rakewell, like Walpole, is now a 'Great Man' and he holds a levee; Walpole's levees, notorious for their affectations, were leading and typical targets for attack in anti-Walpole satire.[124] The more astute and politically educated among Hogarth's spectators would have recognised in the picture of Rakewell at his levee a parallel with Walpole at his levee. Plate 3 of *A Rake's Progress* reveals another aspect of the luxurious lifestyle of

Rakewell, his squandering of money on food, drink, tobacco and sex. In the late 1720s and in the 1730s the old moralistic attacks on luxury had a new, distinctively political slant. Luxury and pleasure-seeking were seen as the representative features of a country that had become grossly materialistic under Walpole's administration and under Walpole's personal example.[125] Hogarth's picture of the lavish and luxurious Rakewell indulging in the pleasures of the flesh has inevitable political ramifications in view of the 1730s habitual perception of luxury as a characteristically Walpolian vice. On a personal level Walpole had gained notoriety for the bacchanalian feasts he held at his seat in Norfolk; he had gained too a reputation for sexual debauchery – in his physical and sexual appetites Rakewell is evocative of the libertine Walpole. Rakewell in his lewd and prodigal lifestyle imitates the Roman emperors ('Great Men') like Nero, whose portraits decorate the tavern walls; significantly, it was at the time common to compare Walpole to Roman tyrants and Walpole's Britain in its moral collapse to the decadence and decline of the Roman Empire.[126] The politically educated among Hogarth's spectators would have recognised that Plate 3's details of Roman tyrants and its general picture of luxury and decadence, were in line with satirical trends in anti-Walpole literature. Plate 4 contains more specific political references. The detail of the little boy engrossed in an anti-Walpole newspaper, *The Farthing Post*,[127] recalls an earlier satire by Hogarth entitled *The Politician (Figures 47-48)* The street urchins imitate their social superiors (men like Rakewell) in their gambling

Figure 47: William Hogarth: *A Rake's Progress* (detail)

Figure 48: William
Hogarth: *The Politician*

habits, and the political interest of the little boy is also meant to reflect
mockingly on Rakewell's situation. Rakewell is now a place-seeker,
he is on his way to St. James Palace to a levee held to celebrate Queen
Caroline's birthday. (Caroline was Walpole's main supporter at Court
and it was by her influence that Walpole remained in Office for so
long). Hogarth had earlier sniped at Royalty, in Plate 2, in the
reference to George II's patronage of foreign music: the harpsicord
upon which a musician plays the score of an Opera for Italian
performers is marked 'I. Mahoan Fecit' – Joseph Mahoon was the
King's harpsicord-maker. Plate 6's reference to South Sea (the poster
bearing the Royal Coat of Arms and advertising the business of 'R
Justian Card Maker to His Majesty ... royal Family'), as mentioned
earlier, continued the attack on George II. Apart from the unflattering
reference to Royalty in Plate 4, there is specific reference to Walpole's
disastrously unpopular Excise Bill of 1733, the defeat of which was

the main political event of that year. The Excise Scheme was Walpole's attempt to gain extra revenue from imported tobacco and spirits by converting custom duties on these goods into an inland excise. It evoked widespread popular and parliamentary hostility; dozens of prints and poems appeared, representing Walpole as a tyrant. As Atherton explains, the charge of tyranny was understandable since the Excise proposals would have meant an 'increase in the number of Crown officials, their wide powers of search and seizure, and the summary nature of trials for possible infractions'.[128] In Hogarth's picture the paper attached to one little boy's hat, with its inscription 'Your Vote Interest – Libertys' is undoubtedly a reference to the opposition to Walpole's Excise Scheme. In 1733 the word 'Liberty' was a key political term; it was being constantly evoked by the political opposition in decrying Walpole's attempt to extend his powers – the Opposition claimed that in fighting the Excise Scheme they were fighting Walpole's attempt to snuff out liberty and enslave the nation to his corrupt will.[129] There is in Plate 4 a further allusion to the Excise Scheme in the details of the tobacco pipe being smoked by the boy-politician reading his newspaper, and the spirit glass and tankard which lie next to him (they belong to him, indicating that he is a retailer of spirits). Tobacco pipes, tankards and goblets featured emblematically in anti-Excise prints of 1733[130] for the obvious reason that the Excise Scheme was concerned with tobacco and spirits. Hogarth would certainly have been aware of these facts; it is more than likely that *A Rake's Progress* details of tobacco pipe, tankard and spirit measure are political emblems. Granted that this is so, the political import of Rakewell's arrest can then be realized: like Walpole in 1733, Rakewell is a 'Great Man' in the moment of decline. Many of the anti-Excise prints showed the decline and fall of the 'Great Man' Walpole – B.M. *Satires* No. 1937 for instance depicts the overturning of Walpole's coach by a mob armed with staves and spears. The fall of the 'Great Man' was of course a popular theme in anti-Walpole satire before and after the Excise controversy, Walpole's career being compared to the rise and fall of historical villains like Sejanus or Wolsey.

A Rake's Progress then, whilst dealing with the condition of man, and with profound, universal concerns (avarice, luxury, irrationality, suffering, sin), is still particular enough to include references to the world of contemporary politics. Rakewell is not Walpole but he is Walpolian in manner, aspects of his life and action exemplifying the moral decadence of Walpole's Britain.

Some of Hogarth's contemporaries were obviously able to interpret the subtle political reference in *A Rake's Progress*. For instance one poem[131] explaining Hogarth's pictures describes Plate 3's feasting and gathering of prostitutes as a 'Congress', a political term that was distinctly associated with Walpole in Opposition satire.[132] The same poem, commenting on Rakewell's appearance in Plate 4 describes him as a creature of Walpole:

> At Court he sets up for a place,
> To C[hels]ea makes his frequent jaunts,
> And constantly the levee haunts.
> ....
> A Journal now and then he'd write,
> Or a *Free-Briton* coul'd indite

Chelsea was of course where Walpole resided and *The Free-Briton* was a political journal devoted to Walpole: it advocated the Excise Scheme in 1733 – the Opposition called it a 'Paper fit to [shit] on' (*B.M. Satires* No. 1937). After the publication of *A Rake's Progress* (and not before, as Paulson wrongly states), the Opposition, sensing Hogarth's hostility to Walpole, invited him to do a series of pictures satirizing Walpole in an explicit manner, but he refused to be so direct, a refusal no doubt governed by considerations of finance and of personal safety.[133]

Hogarth's work in the 1730s nevertheless continues to reflect upon aspects of Walpolian politics, albeit in oblique ways.Before *A Rake's Progress* Plate 4, Hogarth had glanced at the Excise controversy in his *Midnight Modern Conversation* engraving of 1733 (*Figure 49*) There, the

Figure 49: William Hogarth: *A Midnight Modern Conversation* (detail)

drunken man on the far right has in his pockets two newspapers, *The London Journal* and *The Craftsman*. He smokes a tobacco pipe and a broken tobacco pipe lies at his feet. Wine and spirits are being consumed in prodigious quantities and tobacco smoke fills the air. *The London Journal* and *The Craftsman* were sworn enemies, one being a paper controlled by Walpole (it was bought over by the Government in 1726), the other the main journal of the Opposition. They took virulently opposite sides on the Excise question. The reference to the two political newspapers and the general scene of drinking and smoking amount to Hogarth's comic response to the Excise controversy of that year – *Midnight Modern Conversation* was published in March, 1733, on the eve of the furious reaction to Walpole's Excise Bill. Opposition to Walpole's ideas on Excise was already in full swing in the months prior to the appearance of Hogarth's print.[134]

His concern for the state of arts, as manifested in works of the 1730s like *The Distrest Poet* (1736/7) and *Strolling Actresses Dressing in a Barn* (1738), can also be seen as having an anti-Walpole slant. In 1737 Parliament passed the Theatre Licensing Act, a measure designed to censor playwrights and to curtail the production of plays hostile to Walpole's administration. In *Strolling Actresses (Figure 50)* a copy of

Figure 50: William Hogarth: *Strolling Actresses Dressing in a Barn*

'The Act against Strolling Players' (a statute from the Licensing Act) lies on the crown on the left foreground. Hogarth makes the mother feeding her baby rest the baby-food on the copy of the Act, which serves as a tablecloth – it is a contemptuous gesture reminiscent of Moll Hackabout's use of Bishop Gibson's *Pastoral Letters* to wrap butter in, in Plate 3 of *A Harlot's Progress*. Hogarth further shows his contempt for Walpole's Licensing Act by placing a pisspot next to the crown, as if to equate the two objects. The monkey urinating in a helmet (horizontally opposite) is a connecting satirical detail. The power of the State (Royalty, Episcopacy, and Law) is mocked by degrading its emblems: in the middle foreground a kitten plays with the orb; another rests on a robe and plays with the lyre (the lyre being a device on the Royal Arms), two judges' periwigs and a rope (the rope or halter symbolic of the Law); a Bishop's mitre resting on a cushion is stuffed with books marked 'Farce' and 'Farces'. Such contempt for the State recalls Hogarth's earlier mood, in works like *Royalty, Episcopacy, and Law* and the *Masquerade Ticket* – in the latter the lion and the unicorn, emblems of Royalty, are shown lolling in a state of obscene stupor. In *Strolling Actresses* the emblems of Officialdom (the mitre, orb, crown and periwigs) are in contrast to the emblems of the common people which are a tobacco pipe, a beer mug, and a piece of bread. As in *A Harlot's Progress* Hogarth is here concerned with the 'somebodies' versus the 'nobodies'; the rulers of State versus the common people whose energies they attempt to repress.

The *Distrest Poet* appeared at a time when there was widespread attack on Walpole for his neglect of genius and his patronage of dunces and scribblers who were hacks in his employ. The decay of learning and the triumph of dullness were attributed exclusively to Walpole's philistinism and to the system of patronage, operated by his government, which rewarded only those who were servile to its political demands. The only interest that Walpole showed in literature was a political one; in addition he believed that the only writing worth reading was economic literature. Walpole as the enemy of literary talent ('*Bob*, the Poet's Foe', as Swift put it) was an established image in anti-Walpole satire.[135] Hogarth's *Distrest Poet* (who, incidentally, is writing on economic matters) is manifestly part of the general pessimism of the times, a pessimism directly related to Walpole's treatment of the writers.

Long after Walpole had died Hogarth still continued to refer to him when depicting avarice and corruption. Plate 2 of the *Election* series (*Figure 51*), published some fifteen years after Walpole's death in 1742, contains a reference to the Excise Scheme of 1733: in the background is a mob laying seige to the Excise Office, their action, as Paulson remarks, looking back to the popular uprising of that year.[136] The detail of election bribery looks back to Walpolian practices – the foreground signboard's inscription, 'Punch Candidate for Guzzle-

Figure 51: William Hogarth: *An Election [Canvassing for Votes]* (detail)

town' is a specific allusion to Walpole. 'Guzzletown' was the fictitious scene of corrupt electioneering in anti-Walpole satire and Punch was repeatedly used as an analogue of Walpole in pictorial satire of the 1720s and 1730s.[137] The mention of Admiral Vernon's victory at Portobello in 1739 (the two men seated at the table are discussing Vernon's strategy) also refers back to Walpolian politics. In 1739 Walpole was being attacked from all sides for his reluctance to defend British honour and British economic interests by his reluctance to engage in war with Spain. Admiral Vernon's action in capturing Portobello was held up as an example of British might, and Vernon (an outspoken opponent of Walpole) was celebrated as a man whose decisiveness and patriotism were in contrast to Walpole's betrayal of his country's interests.[138] All these allusions to Walpole (which form a backdrop to the moral bankruptcy of the 1754 General Elections that

Hogarth's picture deals with) reveal Hogarth's extensive knowledge of the political situation of the 1730s, the crises that faced Walpole, the charges of bribery and corruption brought against his government, and the imagery employed in anti-Walpole satire.

Hogarth's representation of the materialism of his age then, is inspired by the moral, social and financial corruption that characterised Walpole's administration of Britain. Even so, Hogarth was sufficiently oblique in his attack on Walpole to retain the Prime Minister's favour, a remarkable feat of ingenuity. As early as 1728 Walpole had made an attempt to silence Hogarth by a gesture of patronage – Hogarth was invited to engrave the Walpole Salver which may have been his most financially rewarding engraving commission to that point of his career. Hogarth was also to receive lucrative commissions to paint some of Walpole's family, friends and ardent political supporters – people like Lady Cholmondeley, Sir Edward Walpole, Horace Walpole, Bishop Hoadly, the third Duke of Marlborough, Henry Fox and Thomas Winnington. In addition, Hogarth, with Sir James Thornhill, had pained Walpole in 1730 in a scene set in the House of Commons. In 1734 two members of the Walpole family were among the House of Commons Committee investigating Hogarth's petition for securing the copyright of artists. The petition was successful (the Copyright Act was passed soon after), so it would seem that Hogarth's satire on Walpole in works like A Harlot's Progress was sufficiently disguised, subdued and generalised not to antagonize the Prime Minister.[137]

Whilst Hogarth was able to profit from Walpole and his associates, he was still able to flirt profitably with the Opposition, such duality revealing his remarkably disinterested nature when it came to taking money from whatever quarter. From the late 1730s onwards the political Opposition rallied around Frederick, Prince of Wales, in reaction against George II and his minister Walpole. Frederick came to symbolise the spirit of patriotism, he was lauded as the only person capable of saving the nation from the   injuries inflicted by Walpole, the only person capable of resurrecting the ideals of justice, freedom and patriotism that had perished under Walpole's administration. The most eminent writers, including Fielding, Mallett, Thomson, Brooke, Glover amd Akenside, flocked to Leicester House seeking from Prince Frederick what Walpole and George II had denied then: financial patronage and moral inspiration.[140] Hogarth was to some extent involved in this Opposition movement, if not morally and politically, at least financially. In 1740 he designed the ticket for Alfred the Great, King of England, a masque, written by David Mallett (who was one of Prince Frederick's secretaries) and James Thomson, performed in that year to celebrate the birthday of Princess Augusta, Frederick's infant daughter; it was an occasion which, in view of the Royal Family's quarrels at the time, amounted to 'a slap at the

Prince's father, George II'.[141] Passages of the libretto of *Alfred* had a distinctly anti-Walpolian slant. Its celebration of the 'Patriotism' of Alfred, of the indomitable fighting spirit of the British and British commercial and colonial supremacy, had political resonance at the time – war had broken out between Britain and Spain, a struggle that was seen as being a matter of national pride and commercial sense: it was a war that the Opposition had vociferously called for, invoking the slogans about 'patriotism' and 'Liberty', and attacking Walpole for his pacific, servile attitude to Spain. In 1740 such celebration of the war with Spain was commonly a means of attacking Walpole's political policies, policies that were seen as the cause of the loss of British pride and British commercial strength.

A few years earlier, in 1734 or thereabouts, Hogarth had obtained a sitting from Prince Frederick and it is probable that he painted the Prince (and Princess) again, around 1736, possibly in commemmoration of their marriage in that year.[142] There is no need to attach any political significance to Hogarth's association with Prince Frederick since Frederick's household only became an organised centre for opposition to Walpole after 1737.[143] What is likely is that the shift to Frederick resulted from Hogarth's humiliating rejection by George II and Queen Caroline: in 1733 Hogarth had obtained permission to paint the wedding that year between the Princess Royal and the Prince of Orange, but upon entering the Chapel where the ceremony was to be held he was physically turned out by the Lord Chamberlain. George Vertue, writing in 1733, attributed Hogarth's rejection to the action of his rival William Kent (Kent who in the end designed the print of the wedding ceremony); according to Vertue it was Kent's revenge upon Hogarth for being mocked in prints like *Masquerades and Operas*. Vertue also held the opinion that Hogarth's rejection was due to other causes – 'some other causes relating to Sir James Thornhill, whose daughter is marry'd to Mr Hogarth, and is blended with interest & spirit of opposition'.[144] Peter Quennell, interpreting Vertue's words 'interest & spirit of opposition' in a political light, states inaccurately that Thornhill's identification 'with the representatives of the political opposition' had been a contributory factor in the court's rejection of Hogarth. Peter Quennell's source for this inaccurate information is presumably William Osmun's biography of Thornhill, which appeared five years before Quennell's book. Osmun states that Sir James Thornhill voted against Walopole in 1729 when Parliament approved amendments to the King's Civil List.[145] In fact the records show that Thornhill voted *with* Walpole in approving the increased Civil List.[146] Indeed, Thornhill, who was a political supporter of Walpole, always voted with Walpole – in 1733 for instance (the year of Hogarth's rejection by the Court), Thornhill voted for Walpole's Excise Bill at a time when the Prime Minister needed all the support he could muster.[147]

The facts regarding Hogarth's dealings with Walpole and the Opposition are therefore involved and complex. What can be said with certainty is that works like *A Harlot's Progress* contain anti-Walpole sentiments but that Hogarth was ingenious enough to disguise the political elements in his satire, or at least to make them secondary to the moral narrative. Whilst expressing his disgust at the materialist ethos of Walpole's Britain he nevertheless refrains from any direct mention of Walpole, such prudent restraint allowing him to obtain the patronage of Walpole and his wealthy associates. There is therefore a conflict between Hogarth's *moral* feelings about Walpolian corruption, and his *economic* sense. Hogarth was able to balance one against the other, with obvious success. He was able too to keep good with the Opposition, obtaining work from them, including the prestigious commission to paint their hero, Prince Frederick. He did not however put his art to the service of the Opposition. Whilst being morally opposed to Walpolian corruption he was realistic enough not to see any greater virtue in the 'Great Men' of the Opposition. Hence in *A Harlot's Progress,* if Hogarth attacks Walpolian villains, he also satirizes the Tory Sacheverall. In the *Election* pictures of the 1750s both Whig and Tory are depicted in an unfavourable light. To Hogarth 'patriotism' was not to be found among 'Great Men' (of whatever political colour). The true patriots were for him the common people, the ordinary soldiers and sailors, those 'nobodies' who, 'let what party will prevail, can be no gainer yet spend their Blood and time, which is their fortunes' in the service of their country. 'What did the greatest Roman Patriots more?' Hogarth adds.[148]

Notes

1. *The South Sea Bubble and The Numerous Fradulent Projects To Which It Gave Rise in 1720* (London, 1825). In 1756 W. Maitland was attributing the depopulation of London to the effects of the South Sea disaster (M. Dorothy George: *London Life in The Eighteenth Century,* Penguin Books, 1976, p.321 n.17).

2. *The Gentleman's Magazine,* 1732, Vol. 2, pp. 677, 772, 825; 1733, Vol. 3, p.46.

3. D. Templeman: *The Secret History of the Late Directors Of The South Sea Company* (London, 1735); *The Craftsman Extraordinary...On The Present State of Affairs of The South-Sea Company* (28/4/1732); William Platoe in 1729 published an account of South Sea affairs, in *An Extraordinary Craftsman: Containing a Full and particular Account of a South-Sea Scheme.*

4. George Granville's *The Jew of Venice* was being acted in Little Lincoln Inn Fields theatre in 1732. For Granville's modernization of Shakespeare's play see J. Harold Wilson's 'Granville's "Stock-Jobbing Jew"' (*Philological Quarterly* Vol. XIII, No. 1, Jan. 1934, pp. 1-15). Hogarth would have had the opportunity of seeing Centlivre's *A Bold Stroke for a Wife* in 1728, the year he designed the benefit ticket for Milward who was acting as Colonel Feignwell in the play (R. Paulson: *Hogarth's Graphic Works,* 2 Vols., New Haven, 1965, Vol. 1, p.135).

5. 'A Caveat against Bubbling' – *London Journal* No. 663. (reproduced in *The Gentleman's Magazine* 1732, Vol. 2, p.649). Also see *An Answer To A Pamphlet on Publick Credit: Occasioned by the Bill now depending in the House, to prevent the pernicious Practice of Stockjobbing* (London, 1733), pp. 10, 15 etc: 'Witness the Year 1720, that terrible deplorable Year, and the Ruin that ensued...'

6. *A True State Of The South-Sea-Scheme As it was First formed* [by Sir John Blunt] (London, 1732 reprint); *Remarks On The Occurences Of The Years 1720 and 1721 Relating to the Execution Of The South-Sea-Scheme* (London, 1732).

7. Thaddeus Seymour: *Literature And The South Sea Bubble* (Unpublished Ph.D. diss., Chapel Hill, 1955), p. 221 (William Ayre on Pope); pp. 224f. (Pope); pp. 229f. (Swift).

8. Icarus' wings was a common image in Bubble prints – see for instance *B.M. Satires* No. 1612 and 1622 – emblematic of the rise and fall of speculators in stock. For images of alchemy in Bubble prints of 1720 (speculators boiling and distilling things in caludrons etc.) see e.g. *B.M. Satires* No. 1612, No. 1642, etc.

9. From the verse caption of a 1735 copy of the *Rake's Progress* Plate 8 – *B.M. Satires* No. 2247.

10. See *B.M. Satires* No. 1646 for hungry animals (here, mice) crawling over South Sea/Mississippi treasure-chest. The treasure-chest was a recurring detail in many Bubble prints – *B.M. Satires* No. 1632, 1654, etc.

11. R. Paulson: *Hogarth's Graphic Works*, op.cit., Vol. 1, p. 144.

12. J.J. Richetti: *Popular Fiction Before Richardson. Narrative Patterns 1710-1739* (Oxford, 1969), p.39.

13. Allan Ramsay's *The Rise and Fall of Stocks, 1720,* 1.44; in his *Poems* (Edinburgh, 1721).

14. *A Poem Occasion'd by the Rise and Fall of South-Sea Stock* – by 'J.B. Gent.' (London, 1720), p.11; *The Unhappy Stock-Jobber: Or, The South-Sea Penitent. A Pastoral* –in *Several Occasional and Humourous Bubble-Letters, Written to the Merry Journalists, In the Mad Year 1720* (London, 1722), p.31.

15. 'Convinced of the decadence of European culture and ethics, he fixed his hopes on America.' A.A. Luce: *The Life of George Berkeley Bishop of Cloyne* (London, 1949), pp. 95-96. See George Berkeley's 'An Essay Towards preventing the Ruin of Great-Britain' (1721), in *A Miscellany, Containing Several Tracts On Various Subjects By The Bishop of Cloyne* (London, 1752), pp. 31f.

16. For the 'Screen' metaphor in the year 1721, see *B.M. Satires* No. 1710, No. 1712; in the year 1742, *B.M. Satires* No. 2539, No. 2540 and No. 2559. See too M.D. George: *English Political Caricature To 1792* (Oxford, 1959), pp. 78f. for Walpole as 'Robert Skreen'.

17. H.C. Howard: *The Poetical Opposition To Sir Robert Walpole* (Unpublished Ph.D. diss. Ohio State Univ., 1940), pp. 48-49. Also *The Craftsman,* 14/8/1731, 11/9/1731, 18/9/1731, 9/10/1731, etc. See J.H. Plumb: *Sir Robert Walpole The King's Minister* (London, 1960), p. 278, for the resurrection in 1733 of South Sea affairs in Parliament to embarass Walpole.

18. *The Sturdy Beggars* (London, 1733), quoted by N. Parlakian: *The Image of Sir Robert Walpole in English Drama 1728-1742* (Unpublished Ph.D. diss. Columbia Univ., 1967), p. 205. Also for the image of Walpole as projector and jobber: *Mist's Weekly Journal,* 19/6/1725; *The Bee,* 28/7/1733; *Fog's Weekly Journal,* 29/4/1730; *The Craftsman,* 3//5/1733 and 27/10/1733; etc.

19. *The Ruin of Thousands, The Triumph of One: Or, England's Great V...* (London, 1743).

20. *The Political State of Great Britain,* Vol. XLII, p. 427, Oct. 1731; *Daily Post,* 30/10/1731; etc. For brief histories of the Charitable Corporation see J.M. Bullocks's articles in *Bon Accord* (Aberdeen, 20/2/ 1931) and *Notes and Queries* (4/4/1931); *The Sunday Times* (15/3/1931).

21. *Advertisement From The Charitable Fund...* 28/4/1709, in *Collection of Broadsheets,* Vol. 1, No. 136, Goldsmiths Library, University of London, Senate House Library.

22. *The London Journal,* 18/12/1723; *Fog's Weekly Journal* 17/1/1730, 25/4/1730.

23. *The Free Briton,* 1/6/1732; second newspaper cited by Robert Raines: *Marcellus Laroon* (London, 1966), p. 51. Laroon was, incidentally, one of dozens of notable people who lost money – their names are listed in Dr. Mowbray: *The Report of the Gentlemen Appointed by the General Courts of The Charitable Corporation* (London, 1732).

24. John Francis: *Chronicles and Characters of the Stock Exchange* (London, 1849), p. 52. For the ruination and suicide of victims, see *Proposals For A Regulation, or an Entire Suppression of Pawn-brokers* (London, Feb. 1732), pp.24-25. The involvement (though not necessarily criminal) of Jews like Solomon Fernandes Nunes, Jacob Fernandes Nunes and Lazarus Symons can be gathered from their dealings with the Corporation's directors, as revealed in the inventories made of the latters' estates: *A True and Exact Particular And Inventory of ... The ... Estate ... Of ... Sir Archibald Grant, Baronet* (London, 1732), p. 7; *A True and Exact Particular and Inventory of [the Estate of] William Burroughs, Esq,* (London, 1732), p. 27, 28, 36, 62, 64, 65, 71.

25. A.A. Ettinger: *James Edward Oglethorpe. Imperial Idealist* (Oxford, 1936), pp.103, 105.

26. M.G. Largmann: *The Political Image of Sir Robert Walpole* (Unpublished Ph.D. diss., New York Univ., 1965), pp. 29, 112; David Hume: 'A Character of Sir Robert Walpole', in *The Philospohical*

Works (4 Vols., Ed. T.H. Green & T.H. Grose, Germany, 1964), Vol. 2, p. 395. Anti-Walpole literature included plays by Fielding, Henry Brook, Thomas Odell, Edward Phillips, William Hatchett, David Mallett and Benjamin Martyn (many discussed by N. Parlakian: *The Image of Sir Robert Walpole in English Drama, op.cit*); poems by Pope, Swift, Thomson and Gay; novels like Samuel Brunt's *Voyages to Cacklogallinia* (1727), and a mass of ballads collected by Milton Percival: *Political Ballads Illustrating The Administration of Sir Robert Walpole* (Oxford, 1916)

27. *The Beggar's Opera and other Eighteenth-Century Plays*. Introduced by David W. Lindsay (Everyman Edition, London, 1975), pp. XIII-XIV.

28. R. Paulson: *Hogarth. His Life.., op.cit.*, Vol. 1, p. 539, n.30. Subsequent to our discussion on the subject, Prof. Paulson has incorporated references from this essay in a footnote to his study on Hogarth (*Book and Painting*, Tennessee, 1982)

29. *Bob Lynn Against Franck-Lynn: Or, a full History Of The Controversies and Dissentions in the Family of the Lynn's* (London, 1732), p.16.

30. Letter to Swift, 31/3/1730. In *The Letters of John Gay* (ed. C.F. Burgess, Oxford, 1966), p. 91; Also *Some Authentick Memoirs Of The Life Of Colonel Ch...s, Rape-Master-General of Great Britain* (London, 1730), p. 2. For Walpole as the 'Great Man', see J.H. Plumb: *Sir Robert Walpole, The King's Minister, op.cit.*, p.81.

31.   'To the immortal Memory of
                  THOMAS WOLSEY,
           Cardinal of the holy *Roman* See;
       Who being adorned with a multitude of Honours,
       Which he did not gain by any Publick Calamity' ...etc,
(*The Craftsman*, 13/4/1728; 25/5/1728)

32. 'On Colonel Francisco Rape-Master-General of Great Britian', in Milton Percival's *Political Ballads, op.cit.*, Ballad No. XIV, p. 34f.

33. Also *Daily Journal* 31/8/1730; *St James Evening Post*, 5/9/1730; *London Evening Post*, 5/9/1730. The *Grub-Street Journal* of July 30th, 1730 tells of Walpole's screening of Charteris: 'Knighthood's shield protects the *Squire of Dames.*' For the many links between Charteris and Walpole in 1730 satires see B.A. Goldgar's *Walpole and The Wits* (Nebraska, 1976), pp. 106, 107, 97.

34. R. Paulson: *Hogarth. His Life..., op.cit.*, Vol. 1, pp. 244-5.

35. W.R. Scott: *The Constitution And Finance Of English, Scottish And Irish Joint-Stock Companies to 1720* (3 Vols., Cambridge, 1911), Vol. 3, p.158.

36. *A List of the Names of the Corporation of the Governor and Company of Merchants of Great Britain Trading to the South-Seas* (Dec., 1714). He is also listed in 1712, again with four stars beside his name – *A List of the Names of The Corporation...Trading to the South-Seas* (London, 1712), p.2. For his 1720 investments, see *Names of the Subscribers ...into the First Money Subscription for sale of South Sea Stock* (Box 57, Book No. 1, *House of Lords Records Office Manuscripts*; also Box 58, Book No. 2: 2nd subscription of April 29th, 1720; Boxes 61 and 158: the 3rd subscription of June 17th, 1720).

37. *The Life of Colonel Don Francisco* (London, c. 1730), p.17; *Don Francisco's Descent to The Infernal Regions, An Interlude* (London, 1732); *Mother Needham's Elegy* (London, c.1730) [a broadsheet].

38. *Gentleman's Magazine* 1731, Vol. 1, p.497 – his name is among the list of names of directors of the Corporation.

39. *The Ruin of Thousands, op.cit.*, p.9.

40. N. Parlakian, *op.cit.*, p.69. For 'pimps' in anti-Walpole newspapers, see *Fog's Weekly Journal*, 10/1/1730; *The Craftsman*, 28/3/1730.

41. *Bob-Lynn Against Franck-Lynn* (London, 1732), pp.21f; *The Projector's Looking-Glass* (London, 1733), p.7; Henry Fielding: *The Welsh Opera* (London, 1731) – there, Robin the butler is Walpole and Sweetisa the chambermaid is Molly Skerrett (see W.L. Cross: *The History of Henry Fielding*, 3 Vols., New Haven, 1918, Vol. 1, pp.105-7).

42. N. Parlakian, *op.cit.*, p.91.

43. 'The Progress of Patriotism. A Tale' – in *Robin's Panegyrick. Or, The Norfolk Miscellany* (London, c.1729), p.103. Also *The Craftsman* (14 Vols, London, 1731-37), Vol.5, p.326.

44. D. Kunzle: *The Early Comic Strip* (California, 1973), p.307.

45. E.g. *The Political State of Great Britian*, Vol. XXXIX, p. 323; *Grub-Street Journal*, 5/3/1730 ('Orders are gone to the Sheriff of Lancashire to seize on the said Col. Chartres three Lordships in that County, viz. Hornby – Castle – Ormskirk, and another within 2 miles of Lancaster, all amounting to

the yearly value of 4000 1.'); *Fog's Weekly Journal*, 18/4/1730; *Some Authentick Memoirs Of The Life Of Colonel Ch----s, op.cit.*, pp.10, 32; *The History of Colonel Francis Ch-rtr-s, op.cit.*, p.21.

46. *The Craftsman*, 29/4/1732; see also, for images of civil war, 6/4/1728, 26/3/1727, 2/3/1728, 16/3/1728, 6/4/1728, 5/2/1732, 1/4/1732, 27/5/1732, 3/6/1732, etc. Mabel B. Hessler in *The Literary Opposition To Sir Robert Walpole 1721-1742* (Unpublished Ph.D diss., Univ. of Chicago, 1934) contains many more references.

47. D. Bindman: *William Hogarth* (London, 1981), pp. 78-9.

48. See e.g. Pack No. E69, *British Museum Dept. of Prints & Drawings* (W.H. Willshire's classification).

49. See too Britannia in Hogarth's 'Frontispiece to the Artists' Catalogue of 1761': 'The pretty damsel whose robes succint are tucked up in a way that shows she is used to dirty streets' (Hartley Coleridge: *Essays and Marginalia*, 2 Vols, London, 1851, Vol. 1, p. 287)

50. H. Atherton: *Political Prints in the Age of Hogarth* (Oxford, 1974), p.95.

51. In *Robin's Panegyrick. Or, The Norfolk Miscellany* (London, c. 1729), pp. 83-4.

52. J. Nichols: *Biographical Anecdotes of William Hogarth* (London, 1781), p.90.

53. For example, in Alexander Blunt's [i.e. E. Bockett] *Blunt to Walpole, A Familiar Epistle In Behalf of the British Distillery* (London, 1730), p.10 – he says wittily that he'll show by literal and plain argument, as opposed to using Woolston's peculiar method of allegorization, that the Gin trade is to the public advantage.

54. *Some Authentick Memoirs Of The Life Of Col. Ch...s, op.cit.*, p.45.

55. Reproduced in *Scotch Gallantry display'd: Or The Life And Adventures of the unparalel'd Col. Fr-nc-s Ch-rt-s* (London, 1730), p.35.

56. *The Life Of Mr Woolston, With An impartial Account of his Writings* (London, 1733), pp.25-26; *The History of Colonel Francis Ch-rtr-s, op.cit.*, p.6.

57. Thomas Woolston: *Sixth Discourse on the Miracles of our Saviour* (London, 1729), p.41; *Mr Woolston's Defence of His Discourses On the Miracles Of Our Saviour* (London, 1729), p.58f., *An Answer To The Jewish Rabbi's Two Letters Against Christ's Resurrection...in a Letter to Mr Woolston* (London, 1729); *An Impartial Examination and Full Confutation Of The Argument Brought By Mr Woolston's Pretended Rabbi* (London, 2nd ed., 1730).

58. *Mr Woolston's Defence Of His Discourses op.cit.*, pp.22f. Woolston dedicated his first Discourse to Gibson, perhaps provocatively, since Gibson had prosecuted Woolston's earlier work *The Moderator* – see Thomas Woolston: *A Discourse On The Miracles Of Our Saviour* (6th ed., London, 1729), p.IV.

59. Thomas Woolston: *A Second Discourse On The Miracles Of Our Saviour* (2nd ed., London, 1729), pp.23-4.

60. *Mr Woolston's Defence of His Discourses, op.cit.*, p.70.

61. Norman Sykes: *Edmund Gibson Bishop of London 1669-1748* (Oxford, 1926), p.117. Also Norman Sykes: 'Bishop Gibson and Sir Robert Walpole', in *English Historical Review* (1929), p.628 – on the alliance between Walpole and the clergy 'designed to diminish the possibility of a Tory revival'.

62. C.B. Realey: *The Early Opposition To Sir Robert Walpole 1720-1727* (Kansas, 1931), p.141; *The Knight and the Prelate; A New Ballad* (London, 1734), p.7.

63. *The Knight and the Prelate, op.cit.*, p.6.

64. A later satire on Gibson was attributed to Hogarth – see *B.M. Satires* No. 2281; also R. Paulson: *Hogarth's Graphic Works, op.cit.*, Vol.1, p.305.

65. In the 4th state of the print the Bishop of London is indicated on the letter – see R Paulson: *Hogarth's Graphic Works, op.cit.*, Vol.1, p.145.

66. William Arnall: *Animadversions On A Reverend Prelate's Remarks Upon The Bill ... to prevent Suits for Tythes*, (London, 1736), p.19. See too *A Letter to a Member of Parliament, in Relation to the Bill ... to prevent Suits for Tithes – By a Clergyman* (London, 1731), and *An Answer To The Remarks Upon The Bill ... Concerning Tythes* (London, 1731).

67. William Arnall, *op.cit.*, p.30.

68. For Walpole and slavery, see *The Craftsman* 16/3/1728, 20/4/1728, 17/8/1728, 28/2/1730 etc.

69. E.g. *Common Sense*, 4/10/1740.

70. *Some Authentick Memoirs Of The Life Of Colonel Ch...s, op.cit.*, p.10.

71. *Mr Woolston's Defence of His Discourses, op.cit.*, p.35.

72. John Wickcliffe: *Remarks Upon two late Presentments Of The Grand-Jury Of The County of Middlesex* (London, 1729), p.III.

73. *An Historical Treatise Concerning Jews and Judaism* (London, 1720), p.16.

74. *London Journal* 21/9/1723. For more details on 'the then common prejudicial notion that Jews were exceptionally lustful and that their wealth, when put at the service of their sexual longings, was a threat to English womanhood', see T.E. Endelman's *The Jews Of Georgian England 1714-1830* (Philadelphia, 1979), p.129f.

75. Sir J. Child: *A New Discourse Of Trade* (London, 1698 ed.), p.140f; *An Humble Address to the Honourable House of Commons on the behalf of Traders of England, against Naturalizing Aliens* (1699) – in Goldsmiths Library, Univ. of London: *Collection of Broadsides* Vol.1, No.90; John Toland: *Reasons for Naturalizing The Jews in Great Britain and Ireland* (London, 1714), reproduced in P. Radin: *Pamphlets relating to the Jews in England during the 17th and 18th Centuries* (California, 1939), pp. 41-65; *A Confutation Of The Reasons For Naturalizing the Jews* (London, 1715).

76. Jacob Katz: *Jews and Freemasons in Europe 1723-1939* (Cambridge, Mass., 1970), p.16. Also J.M. Shaftesbury's 'Jews in English Regular Freemasonry, 1717-1860', in *The Jewish Historical Society of England: Transactions* (Sessions 1973-1975, Vol. XXV and Miscellanies, Part X). *The Gentleman's Magazine* Vol.1, 1731, p.5, has an article in defence of the idea of Jewish naturalization. The *Daily Post*, Sept. 22nd, 1732 and *The Gentleman's Magazine* Vol.2, 1732, p.966 discuss Jews and membership of Lodges. See too *The Gentleman's Magazine* Vol. 1, 1731, pp. 76, 95 and *B.M. Satires* No. 1998 for the issue of naturalization. In 1731 a Naturalization Bill was introduced into Parliament – see *The Gentleman's Magazine* Vol. 1, 1731, p.212. [A copy of the Bill is in the Goldsmiths Library, London University, on microfilm].

77. 'On the Bill for Naturalizing Jews' – in *Robin's Panegyrick* (c.1729), *op.cit.*, pp.111f. The poem exists separately, in broadsheet form, a copy of which is in the Public Records Office (State Papers, Domestic, George II, Bundle 5) – see Milton Percival: *Political Ballads, op.cit.*, p.185.

78. In *Robin's Panegyrick* (c.1729), *op.cit.*, pp.120-21. Albert Hyamson in *The Saphardim of England* (London, 1951), p.141, reveals that Jews in 1729 gave gifts to Walpole's servants in an attempt at bribery.

79. Peter Quennell: *Hogarth's Progress* (New York, 1955), pp.95-6.

80. *The Ceremonies of The Present Jews* (London, 1728), p.5.

81. Richard Savage: *The Progress Of A Divine, op.cit.*, 1.52; *B.M. Satires* No. 2140; Mabel B. Hessler, *op.cit.*, p.69.

82. C.C. Trench: *George II* (London, 1973), p.54; Peter Quennell, *op.cit.*, pp.52-3.

83. *A List Of The Names of … Proprietors of the Bank of England … Qualified to Vote* (1738, 1749, 1750) –in Goldsmiths Library, Univ. of London; H. Atherton, *op.cit.*, pp.164, 167; C. Roth: *A History Of The Jews In England* (Oxford, 1941), p.207 n.1; M.F. Modder: *The Jews In The Literature of England* (Philadelphia, 1939), p.47. W. Eden Hooper, in *The Stock Exchange In The Year 1900* (London, 1900), p.34, states, without documentation that Walpole was a friend of Gideon.

84. *The Jew Decoy'd; Or, The Progress Of A Harlot* (London, 1735), p.27; J.D. Breval: *The Lure of Venus: Or, A Harlot's Progress* (London, 1733), pp. 28-9.

85. John Philipps: *Titles and Honours Conferred by His Late Majesty King George I. And His present Majesty, In Great-Britain and Ireland* (London, 1728), p.6.

86. For example, *The Charge delivered by William Cowper, Esq; At the Sessions of the Peace and Oyer and Terminer, For the County of Middlesex, To The Grand Jury and Other Juries* (London, 1730).

87. Sir John Gonson: *Sir John Gonson's Five Charges To Several Grand Juries* (London, 1730) pp.45, 49f. Each Charge was also published separately. The 1730 edition cited here is the third edition of Gonson's *Charges*.

88. C.B. Realey, *op.cit.*, p.146; for the Freedom of the Press debate and the many prosecutions of political writers and printers, see Realey, *op.cit.*, pp.147, 209, 210; also *The Craftsman*, 28/9/1728; 12/10/1728, 26/10/1728, 30/11/1728, 28/3/1730 etc.

89. B.A. Goldgar, *op.cit.*, p.65.

90. *Fog's Weekly Journal* 28/3/1730. Gonson and the affidavit is mentioned again in a satirical correspondence from 'John English' in *Fog's Weekly Journal* No. 84 – May 2nd, 1730. See too *The Craftsman* No. 195 – 28/3/1730. For the Dunkirk controversy, see *Fog's Weekly Journal*, 28/3/1730, 14/3/1730, 28/3/1730, 4/4/1730 etc. Also Viscount Bolinbroke's *The case of Dunkirk Faithfully Stated, And Impartially Considered* (London, 1730); *A Summary Account of the State of Dunkirk and the Negociations*

relating thereto (London, 1730). The subject inspired a popular ballad, *The Saylor's Song, or D-nk--k restored* (1730).

91. *Mr Woolston's Defence of His Discourses, op.cit.*, p.9; *Sir John Gonson's Five Charges, op.cit.*, p.27.

92. 'A true Copy of a List of Fifteen proposed to Inspect the Affairs of the South-Sea Company' – in *Robin's Panegyrick. Or, the Norfolk Miscellany Part III* (London, n.d.), p.133.

93. *Scotch Gallantry display'd, op.cit.*, pp.10-12.

94. *Fog's Weekly Journal*, 18/4/1730; *The Gentleman's Magazine*, 1732, Vol.2, p.678; Sir J. Gonson: *Five Charges, op.cit.*, p.12.

95. R. Paulson: *Hogarth. His Life, op.cit.*, Vol.1, p.257.

96. *Fog's Weekly Journal* 6/3/1731. The previous month saw the release of two petty thieves who had attempted to burgle Walpole's house at Chelsea and who had served 2 years in prison for their deeds. Meanwhile, cynical minds would have concluded, the great thief Walpole was plundering the Nation with impunity. (See *Fog's Weekly Journal*, 6/2/1731)

97. *The Historical Register*, 1733, No. LXX, p.140.

98. *Scotch Gallantry display'd, op.cit.*, p.23; R. Paulson: *Hogarth's Graphic Works, op.cit.*, Vol.1, p.144.

99. *Fog's Weekly Journal*, 5/12/1730; *The Political State of Great Britain*, 1730, Vol. XI, pp.203, 502.

100. *The Political State of Great Britain*, 1730, Vol. XL, pp.502, 592, 593.

101. *The Craftsman*, 5/6/1731: Robert Walpole compared to robbers like Robin Hood, Rob Roy etc; *The Craftsman*, 19/6/1732: 'What reasons can We have to supose that a Man, who plunders a whole Nation without Remorse, would not in a lower Sphere, pick a Pocket, or take a Purse on the Road...?'

102. George Vertue: *Notebooks* (Walpole Society, Oxford, 1929 –), III, p.50.

103. *The Prisoner's Advocate, or, A Caveat Against Under Sheriffs, and their Officers; Jayl-Keepers, and their Agents*, by 'Philalethes' (London, 1726), p.30. *A Report From the Committee Appointed To Enquire Into The State of the Goals of this Kingdom: Relating to the Marshalsea Prison; And farther Relating to the Fleet Prison. With the Resolution of the House of Commons thereupon* (London, 1729). *The Committee's Memorial* (London, 1729); *The Miseries of Goals* [sic], *And The Cruelty of Goalers* (London, 1729); 'W.R.': *The Arbitrary Punishments and Cruel Tortures Inflicted on Prisoners for Debt Represented and Described* (London, 1729).

104. *Fog's Weekly Journal*, 5/12/1730 (Huggins); *ibid.*, 12/12/1730 (Charteris); *The Political State of Great-Britain*, 1730, Vol. XL, pp. 543-4 (Moll Freeman); *Fog's Weekly Journal*, 31/1/1730 (Robert Castell); *ibid.*, 24/1/1730 (James Dalton); *ibid.*, 7/3/1730 (Francis Hackabout); *The Life of Mr Woolston, op.cit.*, p.14.

105 *Mercers Hall. A List of the Names of the Subscribers for Raising the Summe of One Million Sterling, as a Fund for Insuring Ships and Merchandise at Sea* (London, 1718); *The Names of the Subscribers and the Sums Subscribed ... for Sale of South Sea Stock* (June 17th 1720) – Box 61, House of Lords Record Office; *A List of the Corporation ... Trading to the South-Seas, and other Parts of America* (December 25th, 1723), p.6; *An Alphabetical List of the Commissioners appointed by two Acts of Parliament for Building a Bridge ... to Putney* [British Library: 515 1.15 (10); dated c.1727]; *Gentleman's Magazine*, 1734, Vol. 4, p.704. Gonson incidentally was an ageing bachelor at the time of his persecution of youthful women like Moll Hackabout; he managed to get married to a 'Miss Smith' in 1741 (*The Gentleman's Magazine* 1741, Vol. XI, p.665).

106. For the sexual abuse of female prisoners, see *The Jew Decoy'd, op.cit.*, p.30 (Flogwell going off to ravish an inmate); also *The Arbitray Punishments and Cruel Fortunes ... on Prisoners, op. cit.*, p.7 (on the women 'shamefully abus'd by the turnkeys, insomuch that some have dy'd of the wounds and hurts they have received.')

107. Eric Williams: *Capitalism and Slavery* (London. 1964 ed.), pp. 14-15.

108. W.H. Blumenthal: *Brides From Bridewell* (Vermont, 1962), p.54. Hogarth would have known those facts from his merchant acquaintants like William Tothall (a close friend) who in the 1720s was a Westindian sailor, a rum and brandy tradesman, and spent much time in the colonies. See *Hogarth's Peregrination* (ed. Charles Mitchell, Oxford, 1952), p. XVII.

109. *The Political State of Great-Britain* Vol. XLI, p. 414, April 1731. The term 'vermin' had been used in an earlier issue (Vol. XL, p. 501, No. 1730). For Gonson's prosecution of mutilated beggars seeking alms from pregnant gentlewomen as they came out from Church, see *Gentlemen's Magazine* Vol. 1, 1731, p. 401.

110. *The Political State of Great-Britain* Vol. Xl. p. 502, Nov. 1730. For an example of Gonson's own

pious pronouncements on 'industry' see *The Charge Of Sir John Gonson Knt To The Grand Jury Of The Royalty of The Tower of London* (London, 1728), p.23.

111. M. Dorothy George: *English Political Caricature, op.cit.,* p.83.

112. *The Craftsman,* 12/12/1726, 23/12/1726, 20/3/1727, 27/5/1727, 17/6/1727, 15/7/1727, *etc.* For ballads, see 'A World of Quacks; or All Men Turn'd Physicians' and 'The Quack Triumphant', in Milton Percival's *Political Ballads, op.cit.* For plays, see *The Court Legacy* (London, 1733, dedicated to Madam Pulteney, the wife of one of the leaders of the Opposition), in which Walpole is Sir Sidrophel. Finally, *B.M. Satires* No. 1931.

113. *The Bee,* 4/8/1733; *The Craftsman,* 4/5/1728, 15/6/1728.

114. Details of the Forage Contract scandal are given, *inter alia,* in *Mr Walpole's Case, In A Letter From A Tory Member of Parliament, To His Friend in the Country* (London, 1712, Reprinted, 1739). See J.H. Plumb: *Sir Robert Walpole. The Making of a Statesman* (London, 1956), pp. 178-182.

115. *Fog's Weekly Journal,* 9/10/1731; also reproduced in the *Gentleman's Magazine* Vol. 1, 1731, p.421 (Oct. 1731). The forage fraud is mentioned too in *The Gentlemen's Magazine,* 1731, Vol. 1, pp. 248, 342; in William Pulteney's *An Answer to One Part of a late Infamous Libel* (London, 1731), p.43, as one of the frauds perpetrated by Walpole, and, again in 1731, in *The Craftsman,* 14/8/1731, 21/8/1731. Up to the very end of Walpole's career, the forage scandal was being recalled to embarass him: *The Champion,* 17/5/1740 and 10/6/1740; *B.M. Satires* No. 2352, No. 2420, No. 2559.

116. R. Paulson: *Hogarth: His Life ... op.cit.,* Vol. 1, p.174; Derek Jarrett: *The Ingenious Mr Hogarth* (London, 1976), p.65f. Paulson sees a dramatic change in Hogarth's political output from 1728. According to Paulson, prints of the 1720s like *Royalty, Episcopacy, and Law* and *Henry VIII and Anne Boleyn* 'are the last tangible evidence of Hogarth's reactions to politics until the mid-1750s'. M. Dorothy George writes that 'After 1724 none of his prints conforms to the anti-ministerial convention' (*English Political Caricature To 1792, op.cit.,* p.113).

117. See for example, *The Craftsman,* 9/3/1728, 16/3/1728, 23/3/1728.

118. *The Craftsman,* 10/3/1732-3. As Peter Quennell says, Hogarth's 'name and fame were becoming familiar to journalists' around this period (*Hogarth's Progress, op.cit.,* p.120). Incidentally, interpreters of the *Harlot's Progress* like 'Joseph Gay' (i.e. Breval) did sense the anti-Walpole mood of Hogarth's series – 'Joseph Gay' digs at Walpole in describing Hogarth's Jew of Plate 2 as being 'Rich as a Lord, or Minister of State'; also in describing Moll Hackabout's simple ancestry – 'No Titles did her Family adorn ... Nor gap'd for Ribbons red, or Garters blue ...' (*The Lure of Venus, op.cit.,* pp.18, 2-3). On the whole Grub Street overlooked the political elements in Hogarth's series, concentrating almost wholly on the moralistic and the bawdy.

119. *The Bee* 28/4/1733, p.511; *The Craftsman,* 21/4/1733; *The London Magazine* for April 1733 also advertised the poem, according to D. Foxon (*English Verse 1700-1750,* 2 Vols., Cambridge, 1975, Vol.1, p.648).

120. W.L. Cross: *The History Of Henry Fielding* (3 Vols., New Haven, 1918), Vol.1, p.103; J.H.Plumb: *The First Four Georges* (London, 1956), p.76; Goldgar however disagrees on the politics of Gay's play (*Walpole And The Wits, op.cit.,*p.104f.)

121. See F. Antal: *Hogarth and his Place in European Art* (London, 1962), p.219 n.16.

122. E.g. *The Bee* No.21, 1733, p.897; *The Freeholder's Journal,* 6/6/1722. See too H.M. Atherton, *op.cit.,* p.207: 'Walpole's rise from relatively modest circumstances to the very pinnacle of power made his "progress" so remarkable and – for those who hated him – so unbearable. Constant reminders of his origin added sting to the appelation of "great man" and made the comparisons to common criminals more amusing'.

123. Walpole personally patronised Italian Opera and Heidegger's masquerades – see J.H. Plumb's *Sir Robert Walpole. The Making of a Statesman* (London, 1956, p.273); Percy M. Young's *Handel* (London, 1979, revised ed.), p.42. Handel (who is alluded to in Hogarth's picture) and Walpole were being linked in 1733 (see *The Craftsman,* 7/4/1733 for the jingle 'Quoth W[alpol]e to H[ande]l, shall We Too Agree'). Walpole's art treasures at Houghton Hall, amounting to one of the greatest collections of Old Masters in Europe, were frequently the subject of dozens of satirical articles; e.g. *Fog's Weekly Journal,* 2/8/1729, 1/11/1729, 27/12/1729, 30/10/1731; *Mist's Weekly Journal,* 6/4/1728. Hogarth, incidentally, was said to have designed a satirical print on Sir Robert Walpole's and George II's patronage of foreign music (*B.M. Satires,* No. 2777).

124. Nishan Parlakian in *The Image of Sir Robert Walpole In English Drama 1728-1742, op.cit.,* p.168, discusses levee scenes in plays like Thomas Odell's *The Patron* (1729), Henry Fielding's *The Modern Husband* (1732), Edward Phillips *The Stage Mutineers* (1733) and John Kelly's *The Levee* (1741). Walpole's levees, 'held three times a week ... [were] thronged with noble supplicants ... his doors

... besieged by beggars' (J.H. Plumb: *Sir Robert Walpole. The King's Minister* London, 1961, p.98).

125. Mabel B. Hessler in *The Literary Oppositon To Sir Robert Walpole 1721-1742, op.cit.*, discusses the anti-Walpolian theme of luxury in works like Gay's *Fables* and Glover's *Leonidas*. See too *The Craftsman*, 17/2/1726-7, 24/6/1727, 29/7/1727, 16/3/1728-9, 2/8/1729, etc.

126. *The Craftsman*, 20/4/1728, 1/6/1728, 2/10/1730, 19/9/1730, 19/6/1731, 21/8/1731.

127. *The Farthing Post*, Paulson states, was 'a piratical paper that vended gossip and news at a low cost by evading the stamp tax' (*Hogarth's Graphic Works, op.cit.*, Vol.1, p.166). The Stamp Act of 1725 was Walpole's attempt to intimidate journalists and to restrict circulation by putting up the price of newspapers (H.T. Dickinson: *Walpole and the Whig Supremacy* London, 1973, p.155). For more on *The Farthing Post* see *B.M. Satires* No.2202, n.1.

128. H. Atherton, *op.cit.*, p.154.

129. For the slogans about 'liberty' in anti-Excise prints of 1733 see *B.M. Satires* No. 1925, No. 1927, No. 1928 etc. See too H. Atherton, *op.cit.*, pp.153f for the cry of 'liberty' raised against Walpole's Excise Bill, and the image of Walpole as a tyrant.

130. E.g. *B.M. Satires* No. 1921, No. 1927, No. 1940.

131. See *B.M. Satires* No. 2198 (the poem being *The Rake's Progress; or, The Humours of Drury Lane.* See R.E. Moore's *Hogarth's Literary Relationships*, Minnesota, 1948, p.49).

132. 'Congress' was a term used in describing Walpole's bacchanalian parties at Norfolk – see ballads like *The Norfolk Congress; or A Full Account of their Hunting, Feasting and Merry-making* (1728) and *The Norfolk Congress Versified* (c.1728), cited in Milton Percival's *Political Ballads, op.cit.*, pp.185-186; see too *The Congress of Excise-Asses* (1733; reprinted in Percival's *Political Ballads, ibid.*, p.69f), and *The Craftsman* 31/8/1728. The feasting that took place at the Congress of Soissons in 1728 (instead of serious diplomacy) was the origin of the Opposition writers' use of the term 'Congress' in describing Walpole's parties at Norfolk (see J.H. Plumb: *Sir Robert Walpole. The King's Minister, op.cit.*, p.188, for the Congress of Soissons).

133. Sir John Hawkins: *The Life Of Samuel Johnson, LL.D.* (London, 1787), p.500n. Paulson (*Hogarth. His Life, op.cit.*, Vol.1, p.290) wrongly states that the Opposition approached Hogarth after the publication of *A Harlot's Progress*.

134. See *The Craftsman* 28/10/1732 to 9/12/1732. For Walpole and the *London Journal* see C.B. Realey, *op.cit.*, pp.147, 201, 209.

135. 'To Mr. Gay', in *Swift. Poetical Works* (Ed. H. Davis, Oxford, 1967, p.480). See B.A. Goldgar's *Walpole And The Wits, op.cit.*, and K.M. Greene's *Sir Robert Walpole and Literary Patronage* (Unpublished Ph.D. diss., Columbia Univ., 1964), p.7 and *passim*, for the 'distressed poet' theme in anti-Walpole satire, and for the attacks on Walpole's patronage of dunces.

136. R. Paulson: *Hogarth's Graphic Works, op.cit.*, Vol.1, p.231.

137. *The Craftsman*, 17/2/1727/8; *The Plain Truth. A Dialogue between Sir Courtly Jobber, candiate for the Borough of Guzzletown, and Tom Telltruth* (London, 1741) – advertised in *The Champion*, 19/5/1741 (see W.L. Cross: *The History Of Henry Fielding, op.cit.*, Vol.1, pp.297-8); *A Letter from the Mayor of the antient Borough of Guzzle-Down, to Sir Francis Wronghead* (London, 1723) – see *The Gentleman's Magazine*, 1733, Vol. 3, p.163. For Punch as an analogue of Walpole, see M.D. George: *English Political Caricature To 1792, op.cit.*, p.79; *B.M. Satires* No. 2539, No. 2140.

138. *The Champion*, 13/5/1740; *The Patriot*, 7/11/1740 ('The Frenchman's Song'); *B.M. Satires* No. 2421; Milton Percival, *op.cit.*, pp.138f.

139. *Journals of the House of Commons* Vol. XXII (16/1/1732 to 8/12/1737), p.364. In 1731 Joseph Mitchell, Walpole's 'humble bard' was singing the praises of Hogarth – in his *Three Poetical Epistles*. For Mitchell as 'Sir Robert Walpole's Poet', see R. Paulson: *Hogarth: His Life, op.cit.*, Vol.1, p.235; M. Percival: *Political Ballads...op cit.*, p. XVII; B.A. Goldgar: *Walpole And The Wits, op. cit.*, p. 76.

140. See Mabel B. Hessler's *The Literary Opposition To Sir Robert Walpole 1721-1742, op.cit.*, pp.79f for a detailed account of the Patriot King idealism centering around Prince Frederick.

141. R. Paulson: *Hogarth's Graphic Works, op.cit.*, Vol.1, p.184.

142. Oliver Millar: 'Notes on the Royal Collection', in *The Burlington Magazine* Vol. 103, 1961; Oliver Millar: *The Tudor Stuart And Early Georgian Pictures In The Collection Of Her Majesty The Queen* (2 Vols., London, 1963), Vol. 2, Plates 177, 178. In the Yale Centre for British Art at New Haven is a study of four heads (one of which is Prince Fredrick), attributed to Hogarth (Cat. No. 98).

143. B.A. Goldgar: *Walpole And The Wits, op.cit.*, p.145.

144. George Vertue: *Note-Books* (The Walpole Society, Vol. 22, 1934, p.68).

145. P. Quennell, *op.cit.*, p.124; W.R. Osmun: *A Study of the Work of Sir James Thornhill* (Unpublished Ph.D. diss., London Univ., 1950), pp. 177-8.

146. *Cobbett's Parliamentary History of England* Vol. 8, 1722-1733 (London, 1811), pp. 703-4; *A Letter From a Member of Parliament To A Friend in the Country, Concerning The Sum of 115,000 1. Granted for the Service of the Civil List* (London, 1729).

147. *The ever memorable List of Those who voted for and against the Excise* (London, 1734); *Cobbett's Parliamentary History, op.cit.*, Vol. 8, p.1311.

148. W. Hogarth: *Autobiographical Notes*, in J. Burke (Ed.): *The Analysis of Beauty* (Oxford, 1955), p.231.

Appendix I

William Hogarth's Portrait of George Augustus, Prince of Wales

In 1965 Ronald Paulson published the first complete catalogue of Hogarth's prints which included one not previously ascribed to the artist, *His Royal Highness George Prince of Wales, Etc. (Figure 1)*. The obscure fate of this print was all the more strange because its engraved title and signature were in Hogarth's hand, and as Paulson said, it's style closely resembled Hogarth's. The print depicts Hercules standing triumphantly over the dead Hydra of discord. The allegorical figure of Peace sits on the collapsed instruments of war; she holds up to the medallion portrait of the Prince of Wales an olive branch, and lowers a torch with her other hand. Britannia points reverently to the Prince and the three Graces offer him power and patronage of the Arts and of Commerce. The print is obviously about peace but beyond this nothing can be definitely read. Paulson states his belief that 'these figures allude to the peace that followed the Jacobite uprising of 1715' and adds that 'whether the domestic peace of the Hanoverians is also implied is not certain'. The latter peace refers to the celebrated if short lived reconciliation between George I and his son and heir in April 1720, the month, as Jarrett reminds us, that Hogarth made his shop card and set up as an independent engraver. Paulson in his biography of Hogarth argues that the figure and role of Hercules and the arrangement of the allegorical personages in the print owe inspiration to Thornhill's painting on the ceiling of the Upper Hall of the Royal Naval Hospital, Greenwich, which had been completed in October 1722, the implication being that Hogarth's print dates from 1722. But this link with Thornhill's work is conjectural since there is nothing special about the allegorical representation on the Thornhill ceiling – its general principles are quite conventional and in keeping with panegyric portraits of monarchs and great men. Hogarth need not have been specifically affected by the Thornhill portrait and its paraphernalia of mythical bodies even though at the outset of his career he was keenly interested in the works and fortunes of that artist. Moreover a date of 1722 would seem to make nonsense of the earlier suggestion that the print celebrates the Royal reconciliation of 1720, since the latter event was a dead and farcical issue almost immediately after it occurred, and as Jarrett writes, it is 'unlikely that even the most naive printmaker would celebrate its death retrospectively after an interval of two years'. Jarrett belives that the political content of the print points to a 1720 date, to the reconciliation between the King and the Prince of Wales in April, 1720.[1]

There exists another version of Hogarth's print, entitled *To His Royal Highness Prince of Wales* (hereafter referred to as *The Prince of Wales II*) which has lain in total obscurity until now. (*Figure 52*).[2] It differs in many minor details from Hogarth's engraving (hereafter referred to as *The Prince of Wales I*). The image is reversed and the print smaller in size, its borders cutting out extra matter in Hogarth's work, (there are two mountain peaks in Hogarth's, two church steeples, a longer row of buildings, more curtain and clouds, and the second Grace's right hand is fully visible), thus suggesting that the latter is the original from which the former is modelled. Another striking alteration is the greater emphasis on the figure of Prince George. The medallion portrait is upright, not tilted, and the Prince has altogether a more commanding and dignified mien, this achieved by the fuller display of his figure and his stately robes, and the fact that he exists in more space than in Hogarth's print, less obscured or cluttered by the

Figure 52: Anon: *To His Royal Highness Prince of Wales*

gestures of Hercules, Peace and Britannia. There are on closer inspection several other slight points of difference – the coins are more clearly delineated, the pin on the second Grace's garment and the shape of the crosses on her crown are different, the cloud is more regular in shape than Hogarth's, and so on. However the overwhelming impression is of a work strongly imitative of Hogarth's in finely observed details, and this is most apparent in the areas of light and shade in the print which correspond to those in Hogarth's to a remarkable degree – merely observe the patches of light on Hercules' arm for instance.

The publication line bears the name of 'J. Clark'.We can safely assume that J. Clark was not the engraver of the *Prince of Wales II* print, since not only is his style much cruder, but he normally signs his name to any print he engraves and sells. Thus his engraved portrait of George I, which is the headpiece to Richard Daniel's poem, issued in broadsheet form in November 1720,[3] is signed 'J. Clark Sc.1720' and also bears the publication line, 'Sold by J. Clark Engraver, in Castle Yard in Holborn near Chancery Lane, & ye Printsellers'. (*Figure 53*). This work is the one alluded to in the publication line of the *Prince of Wales II* print, 'Sold by J. Clark Engraver in Fleet Street, the Printsellers &c ... Where may be had this size both the Kings picture ...'. The two prints are twin productions in that they are both royal subjects, engraved after Kneller's portraits, and they are both accompanied by panegyric verse.

John Clark, (he signs his name 'Jon. Clark' in one print – B.M. *Satires* No. 1778) is something of a mystery and has been the source of confusion for some two centuries.Even his name has been incorrectly recorded by scholars – our John Clark never spells his name with an 'e'. George Vertue does not cite John Clark in his list of practicising engravers for the years 1713 or 1722, but there is a 'Clarke' in the list for 1744, 'Clarke-writing. hds' – i.e. a writing master or writing engraver, as well as an engraver of portraits. The reference here may well be to our John Clark, but there is no way of knowing.[4] It is certainly not a reference to John Clark, writing master, well-known for his work *Writing improv'd*, even though writing masters were also engravers and publishers (John Sturt or the Bickhams for example), for according to Ambrose Heal this John Clark died in 1736.[5] He did live in Fleet Street, the address given on the *Prince of Wales II* print, in 1727, but he is definitely not the same John Clark of that print, this being clear from Stationers' Company records which indicate separate J. Clarks, one a writing master of Warwick Lane (1718) then Fleet Street (1727), and the other an engraver of Castle Yard Holborn (1721) then Gray's Inn (1726).[6] The problem of identifying the various J. Clarks is confused by the existence of many such names in this period, of people who were engravers, writing masters, printsellers, publishers, printers and booksellers. For instance *The Monthly Catalogue* lists books printed for 'J. Clark' of no revealed address, or of

Nov. 1720.

SOLII PIETAS — LENITASQUE COLUMNA

Revemb: 1720. GREAT *BRITAINS* TRIUMPH

A Poem on his Majesty's Return, by the Reverend M! Archdeacon DANIEL.

BRITAIN arise, in all your Glory smile,
Your King returns to bless his fav'rite Ille,
Kind Heav'n w'h low th'indulgent Mother's pain,
Has giv'n the Monarch to your Arms again;
Still may you boast of such a Hero's Name,
And deathless as his Virtue fix his Fame.
What tributary Thanks, great Sir, are due?
To You, from whom our choicest Blessings come,
Honour abroad, and *Liberty* at home.
When frightfull Slav'ry shook his iron Chain,
And Giant like stood fallen o'er the Plain,
Britannia mourn'd her lost degen'rate Race,
And a dead pale o'er spread the Matron's Face;
But when she saw her HANOVER arise,
New Joy leap'd up, and sparkled in her Eyes,
Lightly she gave her Sorrows to the Wind,
And cast the burthen of her Griefs behind.

So struck w'h terror stood the trembling Fair,
When rolling thro' y' deep she saw y' Monster near,
Short, & more short her panting Breath she drew,
Whilst from her Cheeks the shifting Colours flew
Till the brave Youth shot swiftly to her Aid,
Her *Perseus*, who with joy the Foe survey'd,
Victorious sav'd, and won the shining Maid,
Letabject Minds in borrowed Honours Shine,
And boast a vain *Hereditary Line*,
Condemn'd to move ridiculously Great,
Or Reign the royal Grievances of State,
Your manlier Glories from your Virtue spring,
Virtue w'h form'd, and meant You for a King;
Tis theirs to take their Lustre from a Throne,
Tis Yours to merit, and adorn a Crown.

Had thus the mighty *Cæsar* purchas'd Fame,
And lay'd the Basis of the *Julian* Name,
Had he, like You, been courted to a Throne,
And made his meanest Subjects griefs his own;

His much lov'd Friend had ne'er his Bow'r w'h blood,
Nor drench'd his Dagger in the Patriot's blood;
The noble *Brutus* had a Supplyant come,
And own'd y' guardian God of *Liberty & Rome*.

A visionary Scene your BRITAIN charms,
And y' lov'd thought her glowing Fancy warms,
In You she sees her godlike Heroes rise,
Majestick Forms which glitter in her Eyes;
Her *Edwards* and her *Henries* tread the Plain,
She hears the Thunder of their Arms again;
Ev'n glorious NASSAU the laments no more,
But finds in GEORGE what Will'm was before.

Tho' *Albions* peace employs y' tenderest Care,
Remotest Realms your happy Influence share,
To calm the jarring World to Thee is giv'n,
To Thee, thou aw'full Delegate of Heav'n,
Greatly intent, You scorn inglorious rest,
Whilst *Europe's* Fate lies struggling in y' Breast,
Her good, her safety all your Thoughts control,
And claim the noblest effort of your Soul;
Resolv'd to set her injured Nations free,
And make them taste y' Joys of godlike *Liberty*.

Long had destructive War with rage opprest
The northern Pow'rs, & laid their Kingdoms waste,
There y' rough *Swede* repell'd invasive Arms,
Danger he sought, and sported with Alarms,
To dire Revenge gave up his country's Good,
And rush'd upon his Foes thro' Seas of Blood;
Whilst here the hardy *Russian* scours y' field,
And triumphs o'er a Chief too fierce to yield;
Dear bought the Fame, and poor is the return,
Which makes y' vanquish'd & the Victor mourn,
Your healing Pity bid their Fury cease,
And spake the angry Monarchs into Peace,
Sullen they seem'd to part & Proud to shew
They scorn'd to stoop to ought but Heav'n, & You.

Thus when of old contending Hosts engag'd,
And all the fury of the Battel rag'd,
Should *Jove* proclaim his awfull Presence nigh,
And in loud Thunder roll along the Sky,
They drop their lifted Swords, his Voice obey,
And undecided leave the fortune of the Day.

Count now your Gains, & triumph if you can,
Ye poor Remains of the *Immortal Man*,
No more of purchas'd Towns and Conquest boast,
O greatly Glorious at your Subjects cost,
Stupid and fix'd your mournfull Peasants stand,
Viewing with watry Eyes th'uncultivated Land;
Proudly elate a second *Dunkirk* rose,
Whose ruin buys the Friendship of your Foes,
The *Gallick* Genius fears the World no more,
Trembling and hush'd it listens at the Shoar,
And fears to hear the *British* Lion roar.

Hail, bright *Augusta*, to the distant View
With Banners crown'd thy pompous Turrets shew,
Wanton and gay the flowing Beautie's spread,
High o'er the subject World erect thy Head,
Whilst guilty Faction shuns the *Hero's* sight,
Grows faint, and sickens at superior Light.
Do thou with Joy thy royal Master greet,
And pay thy willing Homage at his Feet,
Confess the Hand from w'ch thy safety springs
And bless y' best of Men, & best of KINGS.

So when the mighty *Constantine* return'd
To his lov'd City which his Absence mourn'd;
Swifter than Winds his eager *Romans* ran
To hail their Chief, & view y' wondrous Man;
Admiring Crowds upon the Object hung,
And the proud Scene with Acclamations rung.

Sold by F. Clark Engraver, in Castle Yard in Holborn near Chancery Lane, & y' Printsellers.

To their ROYAL HIGHNESSES the young PRINCESSES,
this Plate is most Humbly Inscrib'd.

Figure 53: J. Clarke:
George I

Duck Lane near West Smithfield, 'John Clark' of the Bible under the Royal Exchange in Cornhill, 'John Clark' of the Bible and Crown in the Poultry, and so on. Horace Walpole in 1763 lists a Scottish engraver 'John Clarke' (d.1697) who did profile heads of William and Mary, a portrait of Dr Humphrey Prideaux and vignettes for the quarto edition of Lord Lansdowne's works. In the 1782 edition of his *Anecdotes of Painting in England* however there is an added entry relating to our John Clark, spelt 'Clarke', by Walpole: 'There was another John Clarke, who lived in Gray's Inn; he engraved a quarto print of Rubens, and, probably, the plates for Bundy's translation of Catrou, and Rouille's Roman History, and the vignettes for Lord Lansdowne's works'.[7] The last reference here to the vignettes contradicts Walpole's previous attribution of them to John Clarke the Scotsman. Moreover Walpole is wrong from the start to attribute the Prideaux portrait to the Scottish engraver when the dates are so patently incongruous and when the portrait, dated 1722, is clearly signed in the hand of the London engraver, 'J. Clark sculp. 1722.'[8] Joseph Strutt's dictionary has a brief note on 'John Clarke', our London engraver, which is a shortened version of Walpole's entry; Samuel Redgrave and then Bryan both state that John Clark (spelt 'Clarke') worked in the latter part of the seventeenth century, obviously confusing him with the Scottish engraver. Bénézit who spells the name correctly states that John Clark worked in London between 1710-1720, no doubt following the dates given in the Thieme-Becker catalogue; the latter in a lengthy entry confesses uncertainty over the works of 'John Clarke' the Scotsman and 'John Clark' the Londoner. M.H. Grant lists a J. Clark ('this otherwise unknown etcher') operating in 1722 who depicted a battle scene in the Low Countries probably done after J. Wyck or some other recorder of Marlborough's campaigns. Ronald Paulson mentions John Clark as a 'printseller' and gives a 1727 date. Mallet avoids the problems of date and authorship by omitting John Clark altogether.[9] A final example of misleading information is to be found in Hake's index to O'Donoghue's *Catalogue of Engraved British Portraits ... in the British Museum* where 'J. Clark' is listed as the engraver of the portraits of Duncan Campbell, the 4th Earl of Devonshire, George I and William III whilst 'J. Clarke' is listed for the portrait of Humphrey Prideaux.The Prideaux attribution here is again wrong, and even the date of this portrait given by O'Donoghue, '1772', is a misreading of '1722'. It is also evident from style and signature that the J. Clark who engraved the George I, Duncan Campbell and 4th Earl of Devonshire portraits (he gives his address as Castle Yard, Holborn in all three, the first two dating in 1720, the third undateable) is not the same engraver of the William III portrait which is dated 1690.

What can be said with certainty is that John Clark of the *Prince of Wales II* print operated between 1720 and 1736, the earliest traceable print sold by him being the King George portrait (November 1720) at his shop in Castle Yard, Holborn, the latest being *B.M. Satires* No. 2277 entitled *The Funeral Procession of Madam Geneva* (1736) at his shop in Gray's Inn. He moved to Gray's Inn by November 1726 (a date obtained from one of his prints of that year and confirmed by the records of the Stationers' Company)[10] and remained at that address for several years. In 1727 he was selling Hogarth's print, *Music Introduced to Apollo by Minerva* at the Gray's Inn address. Another print, *The Landing of Senesino* (*B.M. Satires* No. 1694) dates from 1727 and not 1720 as the *British Museum Catalogue* claims, this deducible from its publication line, 'Sold by J. Clark Engraver & Printseller in Grays Inn.'; Clark was not in Gray's Inn in 1720 but in Castle Yard, Holborn. There is also internal evidence for the later date of 1727: the two females who rush to receive Senesino make sense only in the context of the rivalry between Cuzzoni and Faustina for the favours of the 'Charming Demi-Man', a rivalry which erupted in 1727 when Senesino returned to England from Italy after recuperating from an illness,[11] and it is this second landing, not the first of 1720, that the print alludes to.

As to the *Prince of Wales II* print sold by John Clark, the Fleet Street address given on its publication line would indicate that Clark moved there some time after November 1720, when he was still at Castle Yard, Holborn, and before November 1726 when he was operating from Gray's Inn. There is no real possibilty of his having two shops simultaneously since he would surely have indicated this in the publication lines of the prints he sold. Ideally one would have looked to eighteenth century local records (land tax, payment tax, sewer rates and poor rates books) to trace the movements of Clark to and from Holborn, Fleet Street and Gray's Inn, but either these records do not exist for the relevant years or else those that survive are unhelpful. Clark is not listed among the freeholds of Holborn and Gray's Inn, which may suggest that he rented rather than owned property in these areas, or else the property he occupied was not of sufficient value to qualify him for inclusion in the lists. Nor are the land tax records for Fleet Street of much use.[12]

The dating of the *Prince of Wales II* print therefore remains a problem. Assuming that it was for sale soon after it was made, then the Fleet Street address would indicate a period after November 1720 and before November 1726. It is unlikely that it can be dated before the King George print of November 1720, since the latter is advertised on the publication line of the former. As to its relationship with the original Prince George print signed by Hogarth, that too is a doubtful matter. It may be that the print signed by Hogarth originated in April 1720 (the dating that results from Jarrett's argument regarding the South Sea Company and the Royal reconciliation outlined earlier), and was on sale then. When it became apparent that the Royal reconciliation was over, and with the collapse of the South Sea Company, Hogarth's print became meaningless, outdated and unsaleable and needed to be reworked and reissued with different connotations. Hence the second print sold by John Clark with poem added, issued perhaps on the birthday of the Prince, an occasion that provided many hack writers and illustrators with an opportunity to earn a little money. The new product would not be making any specific reference to events of 1720; instead it would be a vague and vapid panegyric to the Prince.

Such speculation is borne out a little by the verse accompanying the illustration,[13] which makes no mention of South Sea or of any Royal reconciliation. Instead it is concerned with the Prince as warrior and dwells on the battle for Oudenarde which took place in 1708 under Marlborough's command.[14] The victory over the French at Oudenarde released a spate of nationalistic poems at the time, and the Prince who played what was considered a heroic role in the fighting, narrowly escaping death, was praised by reference to that battle. In 1720, one poet addressing himself to the Prince, writes of Oudenarde as,

> ....The best Campaign,
> That e'er, since *Virgils,* grac'd the *Epick* Strain;
> O let him make fam'd *Audenard* his View,
> And paint, the Glory of the Battle, YOU![15]

Clark may well have acted upon such advice by commissioning verse to be appended to a reworked version of the existing print of the Prince, the *Prince of Wales* by Hogarth. The verse reinterprets old details in Hogarth's print: the collapsed cannon and instruments of war no longer refer to any peace that followed the Jacobite uprising of 1715, and the consequent stability of Hanoverian Britain after the previous and present century's civil turmoils, regicide and revolution, nor do they signify the Royal peace of April 1720; instead they tell of the military collapse of the French at Oudernade when the Prince's Herculean efforts crushed the French and put to death the hydra of discord in Europe by eventually making the French sue for peace. The Prince is paradoxically both warrior and peacemaker and both these qualities are celebrated, the first in the verse caption, the other in the print's emphasis on peace and the consequent flourishing of commerce and arts. There is undoubtedly more to be discovered about John Clark, his relation with the youthful Hogarth and the circumstances that led to the creation of the two Prince George prints. Their dating is crucial in telling us more about what is still an obscure period in Hogarth's life, the first two or three years of his vocation as an engraver, his financial situation, the commissions he received and his dealings with printsellers. Certainly he would not have believed the rubbish about Prince George being great and glorious, the paragon of heroic virtue – his real attitude towards Royalty was to be revealed in works like *Royalty, Episcopacy and Law.* The experience of having to engrave, out of financial necessity, such an image of the Prince would have shaped his perceptions about art and the propagation of false values and untruths; art and the demands of the Patron and Printseller; the artist and his enslavement by the upper-classes; realities which were to concern him throughout his life.

Notes

1. R. Paulson: *Hogarth's Graphic Works* (2 Vols., New Haven, 1965), pp.93-4; D. Jarrett: *The Ingenious Mr Hogarth* (London, 1976), pp.58-9.

2. It lies uncatalogued in The British Library, bound in a volume of eighteenth century miscellania, between *All the Wonders of the World Out-Wondered* (London, 1722) and *The Highland Rogue* (London, 1723). BL: G13, 782/1-8.

3. *Great Britain's Triumph. A Poem on his Majesty's Return* [BL: 112.f.44(38).] Daniel's poem, without illustration, is also to be found in *Miscellaneous Poems, Translations and Imitations by several Hands.* (London.3rd ed., 1720), Vol.2, p.261.

4. *Notebooks*, published by the Walpole Society, Oxford, Vol.XX, p.11, XXII, p.8, XXX, p.197.

5. *The English Writing-Masters and Their Copy-Books 1570-1800.* (Cambridge, 1931), p.29f.

6. The relevant records are on microfilm in the British Museum's Dept of Manuscripts [M/455 (11)]. See D.F. McKenzie: *Stationers' Company Apprentices 1701-1800,* (Oxford, 1978), pp.75-6. McKenzie lists John Clark (spelt 'Clarke') as being at the Castle Yard, Holborn address in 1721, and in Gray's Inn in 1726.

7. *A Catalogue Of Engravers* (Strawberry Hill, 1763), p.91; *Anecdotes of Painting in England* (London, 1782), Vol.5, p.172.

8. This portrait and others discussed below are in the British Museum's Dept. of Prints and Drawings.

9. J. Strutt: *A Biographical Dictionary; Containing An Historical Account Of All The Engravers From The Earliest Period Of The Art Of Engraving To The Present Time* (London, 1785), Vol.1, p.201; S. Regrave: *A Dictionary Of Artists Of The English School: Painters, Sculptors, Architects, Engravers and Ornamentalists.* (2nd ed. 1878. Facsimile ed. Bath, 1970), p.85; *Bryan's Dictionary of Painters and Engravers* (Revised ed. London, 1904), Vol.1, p.299; E. Bénézit: *Dictionnaire critique et documentaire des Peintres, Sculpteurs, Dessinateurs et Graveurs de tous les temps et de tous les pays.* (France, 1949), Vol.2, p.526; *Allgemeines Lexicon Der Bildenden Kunstler* (Leipzeg, 1912), p.52; M.H. Grant: *A Dictionary of British Etchers,* (London, 1952), p.45; R. Paulson: *Hogarth's Graphic Works, op.cit.,* Vol.1, p.331; D.T. Mallett: *Index of Artists* (New York, 1948).

10. B.M. *Satires* No. 1778, dated November 1726 – the print, engraved by James Vertue, was sold by John Clark. Another print of 1726, sold by John Clark, gives the Gray's Inn address also – B.M. *Satires* No. 1780.

11. Percy M. Young: *Handel* (London, 1979), p.42.

12. *G.L.C. Records MR/FB/3; MR/FB/4. Land Tax Records. Guildhall Library. MSS 11, 316/ 59; 11, 316/62; 11, 316/65* etc. A 'John Clarke' is listed in Red Lion Court which led off Fleet Street, for the year 1718, but not again until 1724 ('Mr Clarke'). In the intervening years a Mary Clarke is listed at that location. There are many records that I have been unable to examine properly, but I indicate possible sources of reference for future scholars who may be interested in following up John Clark. In the *Annual Folio Livery Lists* in Stationers' Hall, John Clark is listed from 1722 to 1746 but not in 1748. The list for 1747 is missing. In view of the absence of John Clark's name on the Livery List of 1748 it is possible that he was dead by 1748. William Musgrave (*Obituary Prior to 1800,*

London, 1900, Vol.2, p.8) lists a 'John Clarke, bookseller' who died in May 1746.

13. The verse is anonymous, and has escaped the attention of D.F. Foxon; *English Verse 1701-1750* (Cambridge, 1975). It could have been written by any of a dozen 'Distresed Poets' armed with Bysshe's dictionary of rhymes. (Byles, Beckingham, Eusden and others wrote panegyric epistles to the Prince.)

14. C. Trench: *George II* (London, 1973), p.12f. The other date provided by the poem is 1716/17, when the Prince was made Regent with limited powers on the first of King George I's visits to Hanover.

15. H. Stanhope: *An Epistle To His Royal Highness The Prince of Wales ... Presented On His Birth-Day* (London, 1720), p.11.

Selected Bibliography

(a) Unpublished Studies

Greene, K. *Sir Robert Walpole And Literary Patronage* (Unpublished Ph.D. diss., Columbia Univ., 1964).

Hessler, M. *The Literary Opposition To Sir Robert Walpole 1721 – 1742* (Unpublished Ph.D. diss., Univ. of Chicago, 1934).

Howard, H. *The Poetical Opposition To Sir Robert Walpole* (Unpublished Ph.D. diss., Univ. of Pennsylvania, 1973).

Juhnke, J. *The Prison Theme In The Eighteenth-Century Novel* (Unpublished Ph.D. diss., Univ. of Kansas 1974).

Klinger, M. *William Hogarth and Eighteenth Century Drama* (Unpublished Ph.D. diss., New York Univ., 1970).

Largmann, M. *The Political Image of Sir Robert Walpole Created By Literary Satire In The Opposition Press 1721-1742* (Unpublished Ph.D. diss., New York Univ., 1965).

Meier, T. *Defoe And The Defense Of Commerce* (Unpublished Ph.D. diss., Columbia Univ., 1971).

Osmun, W. *A Study of the Work of Sir James Thornhill* (Unpublished Ph.D diss., London Univ., 1950).

Parlakian, N. *The Image Of Sir Robert Walpole In English Drama 1728-1742* (Unpublished Ph.D. diss., Columbia Univ., 1967).

Seymour, M. *A Group Of Hogarth's Later Prints* (Unpublished Ph.D. diss., Yale Univ., 1930).

Seymour, T. *Literature And The South Sea Bubble* (Unpublished Ph.D. diss., Chapel Hill, 1955).

Wood, W. *The Annual Ships Of The South Sea Company 1711-1736* (Unpublished Ph.D diss., Univ. of Illinois, 1938).

(b) Published Works

Antal, F. *Hogarth and his Place in European Art* (London 1962).

Atherton, H. *Political Prints in the Age of Hogarth* (Oxford 1974).

Bindman, D. *Hogarth* (London 1981).

Bowen, M. *William Hogarth. The Cockney's Mirror* (London 1936).

Carswell, J. *The South Sea Bubble* (London 1961).

Coleridge, S. *Essays and Marginalia* (2 vols., London 1851).

Cowles, V. *The Great Swindle. The Story Of The South Sea Bubble* (London 1960).

Cross, W. *The History Of Henry Fielding* (3 vols., New Haven 1918).

Dabydeen D. *Hogarth's Blacks* (Manchester 1987)

Dickinson, H. *Walpole and the Whig Supremacy* (London 1973).

Dickson, P. *The Financial Revolution in England* (London 1967).

Dobson, A. *William Hogarth* (London 1907).

Endelman, T. *The Jews Of Georgian England 1714-1830* (Philadelphia 1979).

Viscount Erleigh. *The South Sea Bubble* (London 1933).

Gaunt, W. *The World of William Hogarth* (London 1978).

George, M. *English Political Caricature To 1792* (Oxford 1959).

Hughes, P & Williams, D. *The Varied Pattern: Studies in the 18th Century* (Toronto 1971)

Hyamson, A. *The Sephardim Of England* (London 1951)

Ireland, J. *Hogarth Illustrated* (3rd ed., London 1812).

Jarrett, D. *England in the age of Hogarth* (London 1976).

Jarrett, D. *The Ingenious Mr Hogarth* (London 1976).

Kunzle, D. *The Early Comic Strip* (California 1973).

Langford, P. *Walpole and The Robinocracy* (Cambridge 1986)

Laslett, P. *The World we have lost* (London 1979 ed.)

Lichtenberg, G. *Lichtenberg's Commentaries on Hogarth's Engravings* (Translated by I & G Herdan, London 1966).

Lindsay, J. *Hogarth. His Art And His World* (London 1977).

Lindsay, J. *The Monster City. Defoe's London, 1688-1730* (London 1978).

Meredith, H. *The Drama Of Money Making* (London n.d.)

Miller, H. (ed.) *The Augustan Milieu* (Oxford 1970).

Mingay, G. *The Gentry* (London and New York 1976).

Mitchell, C. (ed.) *Hogarth's Perigrination* (Oxford 1952).

Modder, M. *The Jew in the Literature of England* (Philadelphia 1939).

Moore, R. *Hogarth's Literary Relationships* (Minneapolis 1948)

Nicholas, J. *Anecdotes of William Hogarth, Written by Himself* (Facsimile reprint 1970).

Nichols, J & Steevens, G. *The Genuine Works of William Hogarth* (3 vols., London 1808-1817)

Nichols, J. *Literary Anecdotes Of The Eighteenth Century* (9 vols., London 1812/15)

Noble, Y. (ed.) *Twentieth Century Interpretations Of The Beggar's Opera* (New Jersey 1975).

Omberg, H. *William Hogarth's Portrait of Captain Coram* (Uppsala 1974).

Oppé, A. *The Drawings of William Hogarth* (London 1948).

Paulson, R. *Book and Painting* (Tennessee 1982).

Paulson, R. *Emblem and Expression* (London 1975).

Paulson, R. *Hogarth's Graphic Works* (2 vols., New Haven 1965).

Paulson, R. *Hogarth: His Life, Art and Times* (2 vols., New Haven 1971).

Pick, F & Knight, G. *The Pocket History of Freemasonry* (6th ed., London 1977).

Plumb, J. 'Hogarth's Progress', in *The New York Review of Books* XV11, No. 10, Dec. 16th, 1971.

Plumb, J. *Sir Robert Walpole. The King's Minister* (London 1960).

Plumb, J. *Sir Robert Walpole. The Making of a Statesman* (London 1956).

Quennell, P. *Hogarth's Progress* (New York 1955)

Realey, C. *The Early Opposition To Sir Robert Walpole 1720-1727* (Kansas 1931).

Sala, G. *William Hogarth* (London 1866).

Scott, W. *The Constitution And Finance Of English, Scottish And Irish Joint-Stock Companies to 1720* (3 vols., Cambridge 1911).

Scouten, A. *The London State 1660-1800* (Illinois 1961).

Sekora, J. *Luxury, The Concept In Western Thought* (Baltimore and London 1977).

Simon, R. 'Hogarth And The Popular Theatre', in *Renaissance and Modern Studies* Vol. 22, 1978.

Speck, W. 'The Harlot's Progress In Eighteenth-Century England', in *The British Journal for Eighteenth-Century Studies* Vol 3, No. 2, 1980.

Sperling, J. *The South Sea Company. An Historical Essay and Bibliographical Finding List* (Boston, Mass. 1962).

Sutherland, J. *A Preface To Eighteenth Century Poetry* (Oxford 1948)

Sykes, N. 'Bishop Gibson and Sir Robert Walpole', in *English Historical Review* XLIV, 1929.

Sykes, N. *Edmund Gibson Bishop of London 1669-1748* (Oxford 1926).

Trench, C. *George II* (London 1973).

Trusler, J. *Hogarth Moralised* (London 1831 ed.).

Webster, M. *Hogarth* (London 1979).

Whiting, J. *A Handful Of History* (London 1978).

Whitley, W. *Artists And Their Friends In England 1700-1799* (2 vols., London 1928).

Williams, B. *The Whig Supremacy 1714-1760* (2nd ed., Oxford 1962).

List of Illustrations

Figure 1: William Hogarth: *An Allegory of George, Prince of Wales* (engraving, 5¾ x 7 ins., n.d.)

Figure 2: William Hogarth: *The South Sea Scheme* (etching and engraving, 1st state, 8½ x 12⅛ ins., 1721)

Figure 3: *South Sea Bubble Card* (Phillips Collection, Guildhall library, Pack No. 245, 1720)

Figures 4-9: Anon: *South Sea Bubble Cards* (Phillips Collection, Guildhall library, Pack No. 245, 1720)

Figure 10: William Hogarth *The Lottery* (engraving, 2nd state, 8¹³/₁₆ x 12⅝ ins., 1721)

Figure 11: William Hogarth: *Masquerades and Operas* (etching and engraving, 1st state, 5 x 6¹¹/₁₆ x 7¼ ins., 1724)

Figure 12: William Hogarth: Royalty, Episcopacy and Law (etching and engraving, 7³/₁₆ x 7¼ ins., 1724)

Figure 13: William Hogarth: *The Times Plate 1* (detail; etching and engraving, 1st state, 8⁹/₁₆ x 11⅝ ins., 1762)

Figure 14: William Hogarth: *The South Sea Scheme* (detail)

Figure 15: William Hogarth: *The Mystery of Masonry* (etching and engraving, 3rd state, 8½ x 13½ ins., 1724)

Figure 16: William Hogarth: *Cunicularii* (etching, 6 ¹⁵/₁₆ x 9⁷/₁₆ ins., 1726)

Figure 17: William Hogarth: *The Distrest Poet* (engraving, 3rd state, 12⁷/₁₅ x 15⁵/₁₆ ins., 1740)

Figure 18: William Hogarth: *Gin Lane* (etching and engraving, 2nd state, 14³/₁₆ x 12 ins., 1750/1)

Figure 19: William Hogarth: *The South Sea Scheme* (detail)

Figure 20: William Hogarth: *The Four Times of Day – Morning* (etching and engraving, 1st state, 18¹/₁₆ x 14⅞, 1738)

Figure 21: William Hogarth: *The Four Times of Day – Evening* (detail, etching and engraving by B. Baron, 2nd state, 17⅞ x 14¾ ins., 1738)

Figure 22: William Hogarth: *Bathos* (etching and engraving, 10¾ x 12¹³/₁₆ ins., 1764)

Figures 23-30: William Hogarth: *A Rake's Progress* (etching and engraving, 3rd state, [Plate 8: 2nd state], c.13 x 16ins., 1735)

Figure 31: Anon: *South Sea Bubble Card* (Phillips Collection, Guildhall library, Pack No. 245, 1720)

Figure 32: William Hogarth: *A Rake's Progress* Plate 8 (detail, 1st state)

Figures 33-38: William Hogarth: *A Harlot's Progress* (etching and engraving, 1st state, c.12 x 15ins., 1732)

Figure 39: William Hogarth: *Masquerade Ticket* (engraving, 7³/₁₆ x 10 ins., 1727)

Figure 40: William Hogarth: *Marriage à la Mode* (engraving, 3rd state engraved by S. Ravenet, 13¹⁵/₁₆ x 17⅝ ins., 1745)

Figure 41: Anon: *Playing Card* (British Museum Dept. of Prints and Drawings, No. E. 69, early 18th century)

Figure 42: William Hogarth: *An Election [The Polling]* (engraving, 3rd state, 15¹⁵/₁₆ x 21⅜ ins., 1758)

Figure 43: William Hogarth: *An Election [Canvassing for Votes]* (engraving, 5th state engraved by C. Grignion, 15⅞ x 21¼ ins., 1757)

Figures 44-45: William Hogarth: *A Harlot's Progress Plate 1* (details)

Figure 46: Anon: *The Physicians of State* (British Museum Dept. of Prints and Drawings, No. 2268, c. 1735)

Figure 47: William Hogarth: *A Rake's Progress* (detail)

Figure 48: William Hogarth: *The Politician* (etching by J. Sherwin after Hogarth painting, published in 1775)

Figure 49: William Hogarth: *A Midnight Modern Conversation* (etching and engraving, first state, $12^{15}/_{16}$ x 18 ins., 1732/3)

Figure 50: William Hogarth: *Strolling Actresses Dressing in a Barn* (etching and engraving, second state, 16¾ x 21¼ ins., 1738)

Figure 51: William Hogarth: *An Election [Canvassing for Votes]* (detail)

Figure 52: Anon: *To His Royal Highness Prince of Wales* (etching and engraving, n.d.)

Figure 53: J. Clarke: *George I* (etching and engraving, 1720)

Index of Names, Places, Publications

Accadia, 38
Aesop, 62
Alfred the Great, 140
Allen, Mr., 36
Amhurst, N, 22, 82, 113, 130, 132
Anderson, J, 56
Anatomist Dissected, 59
Anne, Queen, 18, 128
Ape-Gentle-Woman, 86
Arbuthnot, Dr, 92
Arne, E, 120
Atherton, H, 135
Atterbury, Lord, 12
Augusta, Princess, 140
Avaratia, 58
Ayre, W, 74

B., J, 23, 24, 30, 31, 34, 38
Babel, 34, 36
Bambridge, T, 120f
Bartholomew Fair, 46
Battle of the Bubbles, 44, 87
Beggar's Opera, 90, 94, 109, 122
Berkerley, Bishop, 42-43, 87
Bindman, D, 98
Blacks, 28, 38, 40, 73, 107f, 123, 124
Blake, W, 11
Blunt, J, 19, 22, 29, 34, 73, 74, 81
Bolinbroke, Lord, 97
Bononcini, G, 45
Bolton, Duke of, 93
Bond, W, 61
Bowles, J, 102
Britannia, 96, 100f
Britannia Stript ... 37
Broken Stock-Jobbers, 29
Brooke, H, 106, 140
Brunt, S, 74

Bubblers Medley, 37
Bubblers Mirrour... 58
Burlington Gate, 46
Burlington House, 46
Butler, S, 51

Caroline, Queen, 134, 141
Castell, R, 120, 121
Centlivre, S, 35, 74
Chamberlen, P, 51
Charitable Corporation, 74
Charteris, F, 91f
Cholmondeley, Lady, 140
Clifton, R, 94
College of Arms, 81
Collcott, G, 115
Columbine, 48
Compleat Gamester, 38
Congreve, W, 44
Cooke, T, 132
Cotton, C, 38
Cowper, W, 11
Coypel, C, 56
Crabbe, G, 11
Craftsman, 88, 95, 97, 113, 118, 121, 123, 125, 126, 127, 130, 132

Daily Courant, 58
Daily Post, 36, 56, 58
Dandridge, B, 103
Dawes, P, 48
Defoe, D, 11, 16-17, 34, 58
Discourse on the Miracles, 102
Disputa, 40
Dissertation on Parties, 97
Dobson, A, 11, 14
Don Quixote..., 56
Douglas, Colonel, 128
The Dream, 102
Drury Lane, 31

Duke (Exchange Alley Porter), 28
Dunciad, 74

Elephant in the Moon, 51
Epistle to Bathurst, 19, 29, 74, 81, 92
Erleigh, Viscount, 59
Essay upon projects, 58
Eurydice, 95
Exchange Alley, 17, 20, 24, 25, 28, 30, 34, 38, 60, 87
Exchange Alley ... 35, 51

Fall of Mortimer, 94
Farthing Post, 133
Faustus, 34, 44
Faux, I, 42, 44f., 58
Fielding, H, 89, 96, 132, 140
Fog's Weekly Journal, 73, 93, 104, 114, 125
Ford, C, 34
Fox, H, 140
Frederick, Prince, 140f
Free-Briton, 136
Freeholders Plea, 15-16
Freeman, M, 121
Free Masons ..., 55, 56

Gamble, E, 17
Gay, J, 13, 36, 37, 61, 91, 95, 119, 122, 125, 132
George II, 140-141
George, M.D., 11, 40
Gibson, E, 102f
Gideon, S, 111-112
Gog, 24, 36
Goldgar, B, 114
Goldsmith, O, 11
Gonson, J, 112f
Gormogons, 52f
Gourlay, J, 94, 107, 129
Grant, A, 89, 90
Grub Street, 60
Grub Street Journal, 92
Guildhall, 24
Gulliver's Travels, 132

Gustavus Vasa, 106

Hampton Court Palace, 50
Harlequin, 40, 44, 48, 58
Harley, R, 18, 68
Harrington, Lord, 118
Haymarket Opera House, 46
Heidegger, J, 42, 46, 47
Hercules, 19, 21
The History of Colonel Francis Chrtr-s..., 96
History of the Priesthood..., 108
Hoadly, Bishop, 140
Hogarth, E, 17
Hogarth, R, 17, 18, 19
Hogarth, William: Works
After, 90
Analysis of Beauty, 52
Bathos, 67f
Before, 90
Cunicularii, 12, 57f
Distrest Poet, 59f., 137f
Election, 100, 142
The Four Times of Day, 62, 63
Gin Lane, 62
A Harlot's Progress, 11, 13, 40, 47, 48, 52, 82f
Henry the Eight and Anne Boleyn, 11, 132
Industry and Idleness, 97
The Lottery, 12, 40f., 46, 62, 68, 100
Marriage à la Mode, 98
Masquerade Ticket, 47, 98, 138
Masquerades and Operas, 12, 42f., 46
Midnight Modern Conversation, 127, 136f
The Mystery of Masonry, 12, 54f
The Politician, 133
A Rake's Progress, 11, 74f., 100, 132f
Royalty, Episcopacy and Law, 11, 49f., 120
His Royal Highness George Prince of Wales, 12, 18f., 68
Strolling Actresses, 137f

The South Sea Scheme, 11, 12, 20f., 46, 52, 53, 59, 62, 64, 81, 96
A Woman Swearing a [Bastard] Child, 123
The Times Plate I, 53, 67
Huggins, J, 90, 120, 121, 123
Hume, D, 90, 91
Humours of Oxford, 132
Hyde Park, 30

Icarus, 74
Imitations of Horace, 74
Indians (American), 38, 40

Jarrett, D, 11, 130
Jews, 24, 25, 31, 56, 57, 73, 74, 82, 86, 103, 109-111
Johnson, S, 98
Jonathan's Coffee House, 35
Justian, R, 80, 134
Juvenal, 48

Kent, W, 48
The Knight, 56
Knight, R, 44, 50, 56, 74, 88
Kunzle, D, 96

Law, J, 29, 34, 45, 56, 106
Lewis, E, 17
Life of Jonathan Wild, 96
Lillo, G, 126
Lindsay, D, 91
Lindsay, J, 11, 14, 52
London Journal, 44, 45, 47, 58, 93, 137
London Merchant, 126

Magog, 24
Mahoon, J, 134
Majesty Misled..., 95
Mallett, D, 95, 140
Martyn, B, 95
Mead, Dr, 94, 121
Meeting of Mary and Elizabeth, 106
Meier, T.K., 14
Miller, J, 132

Mist, N, 113, 114, 115
Mist's Weekly Journal, 74, 88
Monument, 21, 22, 36, 44, 50, 62, 96
Monument Dedicated to Posterity..., 40
Mother Needham, 94, 107, 123
Much Ado About Nothing, 59
Myrmidons, 112

Nero, 133
Newmills Cloth Manufactury, 93
News from Hell..., 51
The North Briton, 129

Oglethorpe, J, 90
Old Bailey, 121
Original Weekly Journal, 29, 36, 51
Osmun, W, 141

Panza, Sancho, 54
Parlakian, N, 94
Paulson, R, 11, 12, 14, 91, 130
Peasants' Revolt, 97
Picart, B, 40
Pilgrim's Progress, 98, 130
Plain Dealer, 55
Political State of Great Britain, 58, 59, 93, 113
Polly, 94, 95, 125
Pope, A, 19, 22, 29, 36, 37, 81, 113
Post Man, 55
Prior, M, 34
The Progress of a Divine, 108
The Projector's Looking-Glass..., 131
Punch, 138-139
Punchinello, 48

Quennell, P, 110, 141
Quinquenpoix, 56

The Ramble, 86
Ramsay, A, 31, 38, 60, 61

Raphael, 40
Raymond, Lord Chief Justice, 121
R-b-n's Progress..., 132
Rich, J, 42, 44, 46
The Rise and Fall of Stocks, 31
Romantic Poets, 11
Royal Academy of Music, 45
Royal Naval Hospital, 50

Sacheverall, Dr, 119, 142
Satires of Donne Versified, 113
The Satyr's Comick Project, 31
Savage, R, 108
Senesino, F, 45
Shadwell, T, 15
Shakespeare, W, 44
Shard, I, 120
Sherburn, G, 11
Sir Robert Brass..., 95
St André, N, 59
St James Park, 30
St Martin's Lane Academy, 17
Steele, R, 37
Suffolk, Earl of, 93
Swift, J, 13, 22, 34, 43, 44, 132, 138
Sword Blade Office, 86
Sympson, J, 123

Templeman, D, 73
Terrae-Filius, 82
Thomson, J, 88, 90
Thornhill, J, 21, 140, 141
Timolean, 95

Tofts, M, 57f
Toland, J, 22, 34, 110
Townshend, Lord, 45
Tragedy of Tragedies, 132
A True State of the South Sea Scheme, 19
Tyler, W, 97

Utrecht, Treaty of, 38, 115

Vernon, Admiral, 139
Vertue, G, 141
The Villany of Stock-Jobbers, 16-17
The Volunteers, 15
Voyage to Cacklogallinia, 74

Walpole, E, 140
Walpole, H, 11, 140
Walpole, R, 11, 12 13, 56, 88f
Walrond, Mr, 36
Walworth, Mayor, 97
Ward, J, 81
War of the Roses, 97
The Weekly Journal, 44, 45, 54
The Weekly Packet, 46
Welsted, L, 42
Wilkes, J, 129
Winnington, T, 140
Woolston, T, 102f
Wordsworth, W, 11

The Yea and Nea Stock-Jobbers, 22
York Building Company, 89
Young, E, 11